Mastering Magento

Maximize the power of Magento: for developers, designers, and store owners

Bret Williams

[PACKT] open source*
PUBLISHING   community experience distilled

BIRMINGHAM - MUMBAI

Mastering Magento

First published: May 2012

Production Reference: 1160512

Published by Packt Publishing Ltd.
Livery Place
35 Livery Street
Birmingham B3 2PB, UK

ISBN 978-1-84951-694-5

www.packtpub.com

Cover Image by Asher Wishkerman (wishkerman@hotmail.com)

Credits

Author
Bret Williams

Reviewers
Ray Bogman
Eric Hileman
Hans Kuijpers
Fernando Miguel

Acquisition Editor
Robin De Jongh

Lead Technical Editor
Kedar Bhat

Technical Editors
Aaron Rosario
Naheed Shaikh

Project Coordinator
Alka Nayak

Proofreader
Aaron Nash

Indexer
Tejal Daruwale

Graphics
Valentina D'silva
Manu Joseph

Production Coordinator
Alwin Roy

Cover Work
Alwin Roy

About the Author

Bret Williams, after 15 years in advertising and political consulting, dove into a new marketing venue in 1995, called the Internet. Over the intervening years, Bret and his team at novusweb® created the first site with live coverage of a major sporting event, the first car dealer website to provide online customization and pricing, and an innovative rapid-development process.

In 2005, Bret and his wife, Cyndi, launched their first owned e-commerce site, which almost immediately became a leader in its niche. Since then, Bret has worked to research and identify open source platforms that can provide the features and functions necessary for online retail success.

Today, Bret and the novusweb® team continue to develop online marketing solutions for their own company as well as select clients all across America.

Mastering Magento, my first book for Packt Publishing, would not have been possible without the mentorship of Acquisition Editor Robin De Jongh. His counsel helped keep this book focused and succinct. I'd also like to thank Zainab Bagasrawala, the Project Coordinator, whose gentle prodding kept me pinned to the keyboard, and Chris Rodrigues, my Lead Technical Editor who helped fine-tune this labor of love.

Of course, I have to thank my wife, Cyndi. She not only proofread each chapter before I submitted it to Packt, she kept me supplied with gourmet coffee, bite-size candies, and the love and support on which I have relied for over 32 years.

About the Reviewers

Ray Bogman is an IT Professional from the Netherlands. He started working with computers since 1983, as a hobby at first. In the past, he has worked for KPN, a large Dutch Telecom company, as a senior security officer.

He has been the SEO of Wild Hibiscus Netherlands (www.wildhibiscus.nl) since 2010, and of Jira ICT (www.jira.nl), which he co-founded in 2006. He is also the co-founder and creator of Yireo (www.yireo.com).

At Jira ICT, he is a Magento, Joomla, and Security evangelist. His focus during the day is training webmasters and consultants the power of Magento, from the basics up to an advanced level.

Besides work, his hobbies are snowboarding, running, going to the movies and music concerts, and loving his wife Mette and daughter Belize.

He has participated in reviewing *Joomla! templates ontwerpen*, a Dutch book that covers Joomla! template tutorials.

Hans Kuijpers, an open source enthusiast, was born and raised in the Netherlands and has been creating websites since 1995. He holds a BS in Technology Management from Fontys University. In the past, he has worked for KPN, a large Dutch Telecom company, as a developer on the DNS platform.

He is currently working for Byte Internet, a Dutch hosting company that strives to be the best in class on Magento hosting. Besides that, he also works for Jira (`http://www.jira.nl/`), a Dutch company that offers Joomla! and Magento training, consulting and project management; and for Yireo, which publishes online videos and tutorials for both Joomla! and Magento. He is also very active in the open source community, organizes Dutch Joomla! day events, and sets up monthly Joomla! user groups.

He has participated in reviewing *Joomla! templates ontwerpen*, a Dutch book that covers Joomla! template tutorials, and *Magento 1.4 Theming Cookbook*, a Packt Publishing book with over 40 recipes to create a fully functional, feature rich, customized Magento theme.

Fernando Miguel has eight years of experience in Information Technology, for two years of which he worked as a trainee, and for six years as a web developer. Today, he has his own company, Origami Web Systems.

He has a Bachelor's degree in Information System from Centro Universitario Modulo, where he has received a scholarship for Best Academic Performance. He did his Post-Graduate in Health Informatics from Universidade Federal de São Paulo.

Frenando has volunteered IT support work for the AIDS Prevention Congress in Caraguatatuba, Sao Paolo, Brazil.

He has good knowledge about Content Management System tools knowledge, specially in Joomla!, Magento, and Wordpress. He also has knowledge about Magento e-commerce CMS development, customization, and support, and can also work on PHP development using ZendFramework.

Fernando has worked on the *Magento 1.4 Theming Cookbook*, and has now worked on this amazing *Mastering Magento* book!

I would like to thank my mother, Edneia, who has helped me a lot with her advice, my wife, Elizabete, for being patient when I've worked overtime, and my grandmother, Mildes, who passed away but still continues to inspire me.

www.PacktPub.com

Support files, eBooks, discount offers, and more

You might want to visit www.PacktPub.com for support files and downloads related to your book.

Did you know that Packt offers eBook versions of every book published, with PDF and ePub files available? You can upgrade to the eBook version at www.PacktPub.com and as a print book customer, you are entitled to a discount on the eBook copy. Get in touch with us at service@packtpub.com for more details.

At www.PacktPub.com, you can also read a collection of free technical articles, sign up for a range of free newsletters and receive exclusive discounts and offers on Packt books and eBooks.

http://PacktLib.PacktPub.com

Do you need instant solutions to your IT questions? PacktLib is Packt's online digital book library. Here, you can access, read and search across Packt's entire library of books.

Why Subscribe?

- Fully searchable across every book published by Packt
- Copy and paste, print, and bookmark content
- On demand and accessible via web browser

Free Access for Packt account holders

If you have an account with Packt at www.PacktPub.com, you can use this to access PacktLib today and view nine entirely free books. Simply use your login credentials for immediate access.

Table of Contents

Preface

Among open source e-commerce platforms, Magento has emerged in a relatively short period of time as the most popular, advanced e-commerce platform on the market. Since 2008, Magento has evolved to claim its own place as an advanced, extendable system.

Magento Inc. claims that people have downloaded the Magento software package over 2.5 million times and that it is used by over 80,000 merchants around the world. Undoubtedly, most of these downloads are of the Community version of the platform. The Professional and Enterprise versions are premium priced, while Community remains free to use as it is—or as you can modify it to meet your needs.

Unfortunately, many find Magento to be more complex and unwieldy than they might prefer. It's understandable given that a basic, initial install of Magento Community includes more than 28,000 files. The Model-View-Controller architecture of Magento as well as the sheer depth of included features contributes to the complexity of the system.

While millions may have downloaded Magento, far fewer have succeeded in mastering the installation, configuration, management, and extendibility of the system. Magento Inc. doesn't provide direct support or substantial online documentation for the Magento Community. Newcomers generally find they are investing a huge amount of time navigating the labyrinth of files, testing possible configurations offered in online forums (many of which are not necessarily correct), and learning by making lots of mistakes. It's not uncommon to find new Magento users—designers and developers, especially—deleting an entire installation and re-installing from scratch, sometimes more than once.

The good news is that Magento, while indeed complex, does not have to be a dreadful experience. There are thousands of others like you who do share great information on online forums and blogs; the system, once you understand its basic building blocks, will absolutely amaze you with its features. And, of course, you have this book to help you get up to speed in far less time than ever before possible.

Mastering Magento was written to be an Owners Manual for Magento, specifically for those who administer, design, or develop with this platform. Administrators will learn how to configure and manage their online e-commerce store. By understanding the theming system of Magento and basic architecture structures, designers can give online stores amazing new looks beyond the usual collection of installable templates. Most importantly, those charged with installing, configuring, and extending the actual platform deployment—the developers—will realize how the system's programming components connect with the intended functionality in order to give the administrator even better performance, features, and control. Developers will quickly become Magento mavens, shortcutting weeks and months of arduous research and trial.

As an Owners Manual, this book is designed to be more of a reference than a tutorial. While there are step-by-step guides throughout, the book is not intended to be a 1-2-3 guide to installing and operating a Magento store. Its purpose is to give you specific information on the different aspects of this grand platform, according to your needs. If you're a designer, you may not need more than a cursory peak at the chapter on product management, instead focusing your time on the chapter on using themes to brand your store. As an administrator, you'll no doubt find more value learning about managing non-product content than about tuning the server for peak performance. That said, it will serve all those who become involved in a Magento installation to give every chapter at least a brief read in order to understand how all the interconnections of files, functions, and features combine to power Magento-based web stores.

For the sake of full disclosure, this book is not a complete Magento guide. Much of the basic installation and operation of Magento is quite transparent or easily understood through online documentation. However, from my own experience, in order to fully utilize the enormous power of Magento, a deeper understanding and application of Magento's features was not—until this book—easily accessible or convenient. I have spent hundreds of hours researching, testing, and documenting so many of Magento's aspects, that it became apparent that others like me could benefit from having a compiled collection of these processes.

This book focuses on the latest version of Magento Community: version 1.6. Many of the concepts discussed remain applicable to earlier versions, but don't assume the configurations and programming presented here will work. If you're entirely new to Magento, you'll be installing version 1.6 anyway, as there is no compelling reason to use an earlier version unless there is a particular must-have extension or theme that only works with an earlier version. Even in this case, it is perhaps better to urge the developer to update their work to version 1.6, rather than go through the potential potholes of updating to 1.6 later.

What this book covers

Chapter 1, Planning for Magento, introduces you to the very structure and purpose of Magento, and helps you create the most important item of all: your plan for building a Magento-powered store.

Chapter 2, Successful Magento Installation, covers installation strategies in a typical shared-server environment, as well as guides you through initial configurations and backup strategies.

Chapter 3, Managing Products, gets to the core of your e-commerce website: the products you will be selling. You'll learn about categories, product types, and presentation features.

Chapter 4, Designs and Themes, not only guides administrators who wish to install pre-designed themes, it also helps designers understand how to convert custom designs into unique Magento themes.

Chapter 5, Configuring to Sell, is how you make money with Magento: the sales process. From payment gateways to customer promotions, this chapter is all about why you have an e-commerce store in the first place.

Chapter 6, Managing Non-product Content, explains how to create and manage non-product information on your site, such as static content pages and sidebar features.

Chapter 7, Marketing Tools, teaches you how Magento helps you attract and convert customers, through product feeds, newsletters, and more.

Chapter 8, Extending Magento, helps you explore the extendibility of Magento through installable extensions or custom programming—or both.

Chapter 9, Optimizing Magento, focuses on making Magento run at the best possible speed and performance, through caching, indexing, and tuning.

Chapter 10, Advanced Techniques, takes you beyond the standard installation and into some common, advanced techniques to add further value to your Magento store.

Chapter 11, Pre-launch Checklist, introduces an all-important pre-launch checklist to help you bring your new Magento store online.

What you need for this book

The most important asset you must have before diving into this book is a sense of adventure. Exploring Magento takes time, but around almost every corner you'll have one "Wow!" moment after another.

Each reader will approach this book from different perspectives, and with different skill sets. Designers will have a good understanding of HTML, CSS, and FTP. Developers will benefit from having a good working knowledge of PHP, MySQL, SSH, and server management. Administrators will have experience with web-based applications, business processes, and product marketing.

If you intend to use this book to help you install, configure, and launch a Magento website, be prepared to have a web server onto which you can install Magento. In *Chapter 2, Successful Magento Installation*, we discuss hosting providers, but, as I show you, Magento can be installed onto your own desktop.

Who this book is for

This book is for anyone using Magento, specifically the widely popular Community version, to create and manage online e-commerce stores. Whether you want to administer, design, or develop the store, you'll understand its complexity and master its power to forge a powerful online selling machine.

Conventions

In this book, you will find a number of styles of text that distinguish between different kinds of information. Here are some examples of these styles, and an explanation of their meaning.

Code words in text are shown as follows: "Ability to override `.htaccess` file option".

A block of code is set as follows:

```
SetEnvIf Host www\.[domain] MAGE_RUN_CODE=[code]
SetEnvIf Host www\.[domain] MAGE_RUN_TYPE=[type]
SetEnvIf Host ^[domain] MAGE_RUN_CODE=[code]
SetEnvIf Host ^[domain] MAGE_RUN_CODE=[type]
```

When we wish to draw your attention to a particular part of a code block, the relevant lines or items are set in bold:

```php
<?php /*<div class="col-wrapper">*/ ?>
    <div class="col-main">
        <?php echo $this->getChildHtml('global_messages') ?>
```

New terms and **important words** are shown in bold. Words that you see on the screen, in menus or dialog boxes for example, appear in the text like this: " It seems easy when you look at the **Store Management** screen".

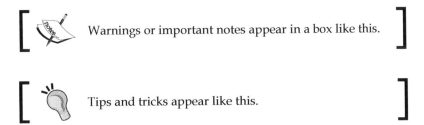

Warnings or important notes appear in a box like this.

Tips and tricks appear like this.

Reader feedback

Feedback from our readers is always welcome. Let us know what you think about this book—what you liked or may have disliked. Reader feedback is important for us to develop titles that you really get the most out of.

To send us general feedback, simply send an e-mail to feedback@packtpub.com, and mention the book title through the subject of your message.

If there is a topic that you have expertise in and you are interested in either writing or contributing to a book, see our author guide on www.packtpub.com/authors.

Customer support

Now that you are the proud owner of a Packt book, we have a number of things to help you to get the most from your purchase.

Errata

Although we have taken every care to ensure the accuracy of our content, mistakes do happen. If you find a mistake in one of our books—maybe a mistake in the text or the code—we would be grateful if you would report this to us. By doing so, you can save other readers from frustration and help us improve subsequent versions of this book. If you find any errata, please report them by visiting http://www.packtpub.com/support, selecting your book, clicking on the **errata submission form** link, and entering the details of your errata. Once your errata are verified, your submission will be accepted and the errata will be uploaded to our website, or added to any list of existing errata, under the Errata section of that title.

Piracy

Piracy of copyright material on the Internet is an ongoing problem across all media. At Packt, we take the protection of our copyright and licenses very seriously. If you come across any illegal copies of our works, in any form, on the Internet, please provide us with the location address or website name immediately so that we can pursue a remedy.

Please contact us at copyright@packtpub.com with a link to the suspected pirated material.

We appreciate your help in protecting our authors, and our ability to bring you valuable content.

Questions

You can contact us at questions@packtpub.com if you are having a problem with any aspect of the book, and we will do our best to address it.

1
Planning for Magento

It's not difficult to download Magento. With some hosting companies, it only takes a simple request or "one-click" to do an initial installation of this powerful e-commerce platform. The question now becomes, *where do you go from here?*

Before you even download and install Magento, it's important that you take some time to plan. The temptation to dive right in and get your feet wet is strong—especially for those of us who enjoy exploring new technologies. However, this is perhaps the primary reason many people abandon Magento even before they get off the ground. Not only are there lots of wonderful features and configurations to tackle, there are significant installation issues to consider even before you download the installer.

 Avoid the "uninstall-reinstall" syndrome. Plan your installation before you install and you're less likely to have to start all over at a later date.

In this chapter, we will learn about:

- How to form a plan for your Magento installation
- How to analyze and research your hosting alternatives
- How Magento's powerful Global-Website-Store methodology gives you tremendous power to run more than one website in a single installation
- How to plan for multiple languages, business entities, and domains

Defining your scope

There are three important areas to consider when defining your e-commerce project:

- Your project requirements (*What do you want to accomplish?*)

- Your users (*Who will be using your Magento installation? What are their roles and capabilities?*)

- Your technical resources (*What are you own skills? Do you have others on whom you will rely?*)

It is never wise to skimp on defining and analyzing any of these, as they all play crucial roles in the successful implementation of any e-commerce project (or any web project). Let's look at each of them in detail.

Project requirements

Magento is a powerful, full-featured e-commerce platform. With that power comes a certain degree of complexity (one very good reason to keep this book handy!). It's important to take your analysis of how to leverage this power one step at a time. As you discover the many facets of Magento, it's easy to become overwhelmed. Don't panic. With proper planning, you'll soon find that Magento is quite manageable for whatever e-commerce project you have in mind.

Magento Go

In 2011, Magento introduced a hosted version of Magento called **Magento Go**. Instead of installing and managing your own Magento installation, you can create stores on Magento's servers. While this relieves you of the hosting tasks, it does come with some limitations, such as the inability to manage more than one website or business in a single backend. Magento has said that all extensions will some day be available for use with Go, but at present that is also not possible.

If you do use Magento Go, you'll find this book to be almost as indispensible as if you created your own installation. Some of the technical information won't be relevant, but almost all of the store configuration and management guidance will be useful.

It is very likely that your e-commerce project is ideal for Magento, particularly if you intend to grow the online business well beyond its initial design and configuration—and who doesn't? Magento's expandability and continued development ensures that, as an open source platform, Magento is the ideal technology for both start-up and mature stores.

When considering Magento as a platform, here's where Magento shines:

- Large numbers of products, categories, and product types.
- Multiple stores, languages, and currencies sharing the same product catalog.
- Ability to add features as needed, whether obtained from third parties or by your own efforts.
- Large, involved developer community, with thousands of experienced developers around the world. You are now a member of that community, and able to share your questions and experiences through forums hosted by Magento.
- Robust, yet usable user interface for administering your store.

Where you might find Magento to be more than required is if you have only a small handful of products to offer or expect very few sales.

If you think that Magento may be too complicated to use as an e-commerce platform, think again. Power always involves some level of complexity. With *Mastering Magento*, we feel the challenge of using Magento will quickly become an appreciation for all the ways you can sell more products online.

Requirements checklist

How are you going to be using your Magento installation? This list will help you focus on particular areas of interest in this book. Answer these questions, as they pertain to your single Magento installation:

- Will you build more than one online store? How many? Will each store share the same products, or different catalogs?
- Will you build different versions of stores in multiple languages and currencies?
- What types of products will be offered? Hard goods? Downloadable? Subscriptions? How many products will be offered?
- Will products be entered individually or imported from lists?
- How many customers do you expect to serve on a monthly basis? What is your anticipated growth rate?
- Are there particular features you consider to be "must-haves" for your stores, such as social marketing, gift certificates, newsletters, customer groups, telephone orders, and so on.

Whatever you can conceive for an e-commerce store, it can almost always be accommodated with Magento!

Planning for users

The second stage to define your scope is to think about "users"—those people who will actually be interacting with Magento: customers and store staff. These are people who have no technical expertise, and for whom using the site should be straightforward and intuitive.

Designers and developers may use Magento's administration screens to configure an installation, but it's the people who actually interact with Magento on a daily basis for whom designers and developers must plan. As you use this book to craft a successful Magento store, always keep the end-user in mind.

Who will be your users? Basically, your users are divided into two segments: staff and customers.

Staff

Staff refers to those who will be using the Magento administration screens on a daily basis. Magento's administration screens are elegant and fairly easy to use, although you'll want to pay close attention to how you create user permissions as described in *Chapter 2, Successful Magento Installation*. Some users won't need access to all the back-end features. By turning off certain features, you can make the administration area much more user-friendly and less overwhelming. Of course, for staff managers, additional permissions can give them access to reports, marketing tools, and content management sections. In short, as you work with staff, you can fine tune their back-end experience and maximize their effectiveness.

One key staff user should be designated as the **Administrator**. If you're the one who will be responsible for managing the Magento configurations on an ongoing basis, congratulations! You now have the power to adjust your online business in ways both significant and subtle at your fingertips. You also have the guide book that will give you a full appreciation of your capabilities in front of you.

Customers

There are several types of **customers**, based on their relationship with the vendor: retail and wholesale. Among these customers, you can also have customers that are members of the site—and therefore privy to certain pricing and promotions—both on the retail and wholesale level. You can also subdivide wholesalers into many other levels of manufacturers, jobbers, distributors, and dealers, all operating through the supply chain.

Magento has the agility to handle a variety of different users and user types, including all those mentioned here.

> The one caveat to consider when scoping users is that if you are going to use a single Magento installation to operate more than one business—which can certainly be done—you cannot create unique permissions for staff users which restrict them from managing the content, customers, and orders of any one business. At least not with the default installation.

Assessing technical resources

As reviewed in the *Preface*, there are basically three different types of people who will be involved in any Magento installation: the Administrator, the Designer, and the Developer. Which one, or ones, are you?

As a complete, installable platform, make sure that you have sufficient technical resources to handle all aspects of web server configuration and administration. It is not uncommon to find one or maybe two people tackling the installation, configuration, and management of a Magento installation. The web industry is well populated with "Jacks-of-all-Trades." As you analyze your own technical abilities, you may find it necessary to hire outside help. These are the disciplines that can help you maximize your Magento success:

- **User Interface Design**: Even if you use one of the many themes available for Magento stores, you will find the need to adjust and modify layouts to give your users a great online experience. Knowledge of HTML, CSS, and JavaScript is critical, and the use of these across multiple browser types means maximum accessibility. As we'll learn in this book, specific knowledge of the Magento design architecture is a plus.

- **PHP**: Many people setting up a Magento store can avoid having to work with the underlying PHP programming code. However, if you want to expand functionality or significantly modify layouts, the ability to at least navigate PHP code is important. Furthermore, a familiarity with programming standards, such as the model-view-controller methodology used in Magento coding (explained in *Chapter 6*, *Managing Non-Product Content*), will increase your ability to modify and, when necessary, fix code.

- **Sales Processes**: Selling online is more complex than most newcomers imagine. While it appears fairly simple and straightforward from the buyer's point of view, the backend management of orders, shipping, payment gateways, distribution, tracking, and so on, requires a good understanding of how products will be priced and offered, inventory managed, orders and returns processed, and shipping handled. Businesses vary as much by how they sell their products as they do by the product categories that they offer.

- **Server Administration.** From domain names and SSL encryption to fine-tuning for performance, the management of your Magento installation involves a thorough understanding of how to configure and manage everything from web and mail servers to databases and FTP accounts. In addition, PCI compliance and security is becoming an increasingly important consideration.

Fortunately, many Magento-friendly hosting providers offer assistance and expertise when it comes to optimizing your Magento installation. In *Chapter 9, Optimizing Magento*, we explain ways you can perform many of the optimization functions yourself, but don't hesitate to have frank discussions with potential hosting providers to find out just how much and how well they can help you with your installation.

If you choose to host the installation on your own in-house servers, note that Magento does require certain "tweaks" for performance and reliability, which we cover in *Chapter 9*.

Technical considerations

You have assessed the technical knowledge and experience of yourself and others with whom you may be working; now it is important that you understand the technical requirements of installing and managing a Magento installation.

Hosting provider

If you're new to Magento, I certainly recommend that you find a capable hosting provider with specific Magento experience. There are many hosting companies that provide hosting suitable for Magento, but far fewer who invest resources toward supporting their clients with specific Magento-related needs. Keep the following points in mind as you research possible hosting candidates:

- Do they provide specific Magento support for installing and optimizing? (You'll learn how to do that in this book, but if you're hesitant to do it yourself, find a provider who can help.)

- Can they provide PCI compliance? (If you're going to accept credit cards online, you'll be asked by your merchant account provider to be "PCI" compliant. We'll cover this in *Chapter 5, Configuring to Sell.*)

- Are they a Magento Partner? (The Magento website lists companies who they have designated as "Solution Partners." While this is a good place to start, there are many other hosting providers who are not official partners, but who do an excellent job in hosting Magento stores.)

- Do they have links to client sites? (If Magento stores are properly optimized, and the servers are fast, the websites will load quickly.)

In-house hosting

You may already be hosting PHP-based websites, have a robust server setup, or manage racked servers at a hosting facility. In these instances, you might well be capable of managing all aspects of hosting a Magento installation. In this book, you will find considerable information to help you configure and manage the server aspects of your Magento installation. I do repeat the advice that if you're new to Magento, an experienced hosting provider could be your best friend.

Servers

Due to Magento's complex architecture, your servers should be powerful. The architecture, indexing, and caching schemas of Magento require considerable resources. While we will attack these issues in *Chapter 9, Optimizing Magento*, the more horsepower you have, the better your store will perform.

To host your own Magento installation, your server must have the following minimum requirements:

- Linux x86, x86-64 operating system
- Apache 1.3.x, 2.0.x or 2.2.x web server
- 5.2.13+ PHP, with these extensions:
    ◦ PDO_MySQL
    ◦ simplexml
    ◦ mcrypt
    ◦ hash
    ◦ GD
    ◦ DOM
    ◦ iconv
    ◦ curl

- SOAP (if the Web Services API will be used)
- PHP Safe_mode off
- PHP Memory_limit not less than 256 MB (512 MB is preferred)
- MySQL 4.1.20 or newer with InnoDB storage engine
- SSL Certificate for secure Administration access (and if you're going to be taking credit card information through your Web site)
- Ability to run `cron` jobs with PHP 5
- Ability to override `.htaccess` file options

The best of both worlds

Most Magento Community users we know (and there are lots!), opt for a hosted solution. Even with my own experience managing web servers, I, too use a third-party hosting provider. It's easier, safer, and, in most cases, far less expensive than duplicating the same degree of service in-house.

However, I do enjoy installing and testing open source platforms in-house, rather than setting up another hosting account. This is especially true when working with new platforms. Setting up an in-house installation can also allow you to test modifications, extensions, and updates before installing them on your live production server.

Setting up a local test installation

You can easily set up an entire web server environment with PHP, MySQL, and Magento, on your own desktop computer or a local server in your office. Enterprising developers have created "one-click" installers that set up a local server instance on any PC or Mac. It's a wonderful way to initially install and learn Magento before committing time and resources to a production server.

These installers are called AMP , short for "Apache-MySQL-PHP," the three main components of a web server environment (at least for PHP-powered websites). *ApacheFriends* (http://www.apachefriends.org/en/xampp.html) provides cross-platform installers, called *XAMPP* (the "X" is for cross-platform). Currently, they have AMP installers for Linux, Windows, Mac OS X, and Solaris. Magento users have successfully used the Windows and Mac installers to create local, desktop Web server environments. XAMPP is free of charge and easy to install and manage.

There are other AMP resources available. For Windows machines, the most popular is WAMP Server (`http:// www.wampserver.com/en/index.php`), currently in its second version. MAMP (`http://www.mamp.info/en/index.html`) offers both a free and Pro version for the Mac OS X. I use the free version and find it very easy and convenient.

After installing AMP, you may still need to make some adjustments to bring your installation in line with the minimum Magento requirements.

Global-Website-Store methodology

Now you're probably itching to install your first Magento store. In fact, you have probably done that already and are fumbling through the vast labyrinth of configuration menus and screens. If you're like so many first-time Magento installers, you may feel ready to uninstall and reinstall; to start all over.

Most of the time, this "restart" happens when users try to take advantage of one of Magento's most powerful features: managing multiple stores. It seems easy when you look at the **Store Management** screen until you begin setting up stores, configuring URLs, and assigning specific configurations to each front-end website.

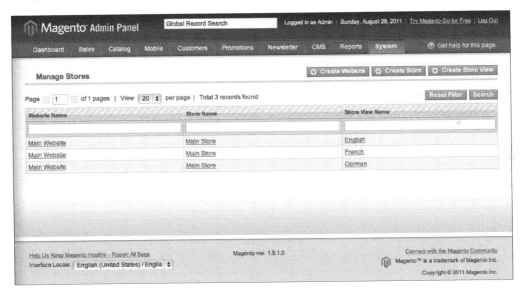

Before you begin laying out your master plan for the various websites and stores that you intend to create (and even if you're only beginning with one website), you need to master the Magento methodology for multiple stores. Magento describes this as **GWS**, short for **Global, Website, Store**. Each Magento installation automatically includes one of each part of this hierarchy, plus one more for **Store View**.

The following diagram shows how each part of **GWS** is related to one another:

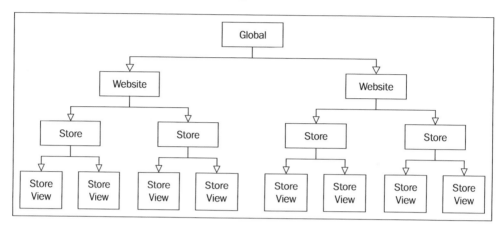

Global

Global refers to settings (for example: stock management rules) and values (for example: product price) for the entire installation. Throughout your Magento installation, you'll find "Global" displayed next to various form fields.

In terms of installation planning, your *Global* considerations should include:

- *Will customers be shared among all sites?* You can elect not to give customers the ability to register for one website and automatically be registered at all others.

- *Can I allow any user with Admin permissions to see all orders and customers from all websites and stores within the single installation?* Without modification, Magento does not allow you to set up Admin users by limiting them to certain websites and stores. If an Admin user can see orders, they can see all orders for all customers.

- *Will all stores within an installation use the same rules for managing inventory?* Inventory rules, such as whether stock is to be managed or whether backorders are allowed, are system-wide choices. (These choices can be changed, in some cases, at the product level, though that does mean careful attention to how products are configured and managed.)

In general, we recommend that you consider a single Magento installation only for multiple websites and stores that are similar in concept. For example, if your online business is selling drop-shipped furniture through several differently branded websites, then a single Magento installation is ideal. However, if you have two or more different businesses, each with a different product focus, company name, banking, and so on, it is best to use a separate Magento installation for each discrete business.

Website

The **Website** is the "root" of a Magento store. From the *Website* multiple *Stores* are created that can each represent different products and focus. However, it is at the *Website* level that certain configurations are applied that control common functions among its children *Stores* and *Store Views*.

As described above, one of the most important considerations at the *Website* level is whether or not customer data can be shared among *Websites*. The decision to share this information is a *Global* configuration. However, remember that you cannot elect to share customer data among some *Websites* and not others; it's an all or nothing configuration.

If you do need to create a group of *Websites* among which customer data is to be shared and then create other *Websites* among which the data is not to be shared, you will need more than one installation of Magento.

Store

What can sometimes be confusing is that Store for Magento is used to describe both a *Store structure* as well as a *Store View*. When configuring your hierarchal structure, **Store** is used to associate different product catalogs to different stores under a single "Website", whereas **Store Views** can be created to display a "Store" in multiple languages or styles, each with their own URL or path. Each Store View can be assigned different themes, content, logos, and so on.

Yet, throughout Magento's many administration screens, you will see that "Store" is used to define the scope of a particular value or setting. In these instances, entered values will affect all **Views** under a Store hierarchy. We know this can be confusing; it was to me, too.

However, following the processes described in this book, you'll quickly come to not only understand how **Store** and **Store View** are referred to within Magento, but also appreciate the tremendous flexibility this gives you.

 Perhaps the best way to consider **Stores** and **Store Views** is to learn that a **View** is what your website visitor will see in terms of language, content, and graphics, while **Store** refers to the data presented in each **View**.

Planning for multiple stores

How you utilize **GWS** in your particular case depends on the purpose of your Magento installation. With **GWS** you have an enormous number of configuration possibilities to explore. That said, your configuration planning would generally fall within three major categories: multiple domains, multiple businesses, and multiple languages. Of course, in the real world, a Magento installation may include aspects of all three.

 It's important to realize that Magento allows you to drive your e-commerce strategy according to your own business and marketing goals, rather than conforming to any limitations according to what your e-commerce platform may or may not be able to deliver.

Using multiple domains for effective market segmentation

It's becoming more popular in e-commerce to create multiple storefronts selling the same or similar products, each having a different domain name, branding design, and content. In this way, merchants can extend their marketing by appealing to different market segments, not just having one website trying to satisfy all consumers.

For example, let's assume that you want to sell shoes online. You have a great distribution source where you can source all kinds of shoes, from dress to casual, running to flip-flops. While you can certainly have a comprehensive, "all types available" online shoe store, you might elect to secure different domain names focused on different segments of the shoe market. *www.runningshoes4you.com* would cater to joggers while *www.highheelsemporium.com* features designer-quality dress shoes for women.

In Magento, you would create one *Website* but create at least two *Stores*, one for each of your domains. You may also create a third as an overall retail store for all your shoes. Each *Store* could either share the same product catalog, or each could have its own separate catalog. By having all *Stores* assigned to the same *Website*, you have the ability to control certain configurations that apply to all *Stores*. For example, if all the *Stores* belong to the same retailer, as in this example, all would offer the same payment methods, such as **PayPal** or **Authorize.Net**. Most likely, the shipping methods that you offer would be the same as well as your policies for returns and shipping.

In short, if all the domains belong to the same retail business, it may make sense to have one *Website* with multiple *Stores*, rather than creating entire *Website-Store* hierarchies for each product-focused domain. As you can see in the following diagram, this makes for a slimmer, more manageable structure:

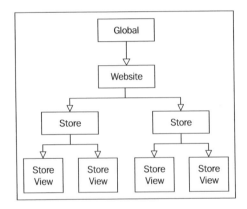

Using multiple businesses to keep finances separate

In contrast, if your installation will be used to manage multiple businesses, you will need to create multiple **Websites**. The reason is that actual, separate business entities will have separate payment system accounts (for example: PayPal, credit card merchant accounts, shipping) and therefore need to be able to segregate these between different websites.

To extend our example, let's assume that your shoe retailer also owns a sideline business selling women's sportswear. This other business exists under a separate legal entity (for example: a corporation or partnership), and therefore has different bank accounts, distributors, and customers. With Magento, you should create separate *Websites* for each account, even if they are to share certain products.

For instance, the sportswear site might also feature women's casual shoes, which are also offered by the shoe website. The same product can be assigned to multiple product catalogs (and therefore different *Stores*) even if the catalogs belong to separate businesses. And somehow, through complex database architectures, Magento succeeds in keeping all this straight for you. Amazing!

 Remember that Magento does not allow you to give back-end user permissions based on *Website*.

Using multiple languages to sell globally

Even among some of Magento's top competitors in the open source e-commerce arena, very few provide the ability to create multiple language views of a website. Multiple language views are not simple for several reasons:

- All site content, including links, instructions, error messages, and so on, must be translated for the intended language.

- The platform must seamlessly provide multiple language selection, and, if possible, intelligently provide the appropriate language to the website visitor based on their geographical location.

- Multiple languages can also infer the need to provide product prices in multiple currencies. Conversion rates vary almost minute-by-minute. Daily swings in conversion rates can affect profitability if the amounts shown online are not updated.

Magento has several tools to help you create multiple languages and currencies for retailers wanting to sell globally (or just provide multiple languages to users within a single country), which we will tackle in *Chapter 2, Successful Magento Installation*. It all begins with creating multiple **Views** for a given **Store**.

In our example, our running shoe website needs to be available in both English and French; you would create two *Views* within the running shoe *Store*, one for each language. In your Magento-powered website, you can easily include a small drop-down selector which allows a visitor to choose their preferred language based on the *Views* you have created.

In fact, in most Magento theme designs, this drop-down is automatic whenever there are multiple *Views* created for any given *Store*.

Another interesting use of multiple *Views* could be to segment your customer market within a *Store*. For example, if you wanted your shoe store to have a different overall look for men versus women versus children, you could create multiple *Views* for each customer segment, then allow the visitor to choose their desired view.

Summary

The power of Magento can also be a curse, particularly if you're like many of us: eager to jump in and begin building an online store. However—and this comes from the experience of wasting lots of hours—taking a moment to understand the scope of your undertaking will make navigating the intricacies of Magento a much more rewarding experience.

In this chapter, we did the following:

- Outlined the key areas to consider when planning our Magento installation
- Understood the powerful Global-Website-Store methodology for managing multiple web stores in a single installation
- Looked at the possibilities of introducing multiple languages, businesses, and domains for effective market segmentation

As we go forward in this book, we'll learn how each decision that we make while installing, configuring, and managing Magento traces back to what we covered in this chapter. In the next chapter, we will be taking your plans from this chapter and applying them to a new Magento installation.

2
Successful Magento Installation

Now that you've got your plan in hand from *Chapter 1, Planning for Magento*, it's time to now take the leap and install **Magento Community**. While some hosting providers will install Magento for you, or provide installation assistance, Magento makes installing fairly easy. There are a few points to pay attention to, but if you follow the steps in this chapter, you will be up and running with Magento in quick order.

In this chapter, we will learn:

- Installation strategies to improve Magento performance
- How to configure multiple websites and stores
- Strategies for backups and security

How hosting affects installation

If you own and operate your own servers, and your server meets the requirements for installing Magento, you are set to go. However, for most people installing Magento Community, the quest to install Magento on an appropriate hosted server is vital to ensure that their Magento stores run fast and secure.

How is a website hosted?

If this is your first time to install, configure, and manage a web-based application of your own, let's take a moment to explain how the various components of running a Magento store fit together.

To serve an e-commerce website, the following are the high-level necessities:

- **Server**: As you probably already know, a physical computer is needed to respond to requests from website visitors and deliver the pages of expected results.

- **Web server**: On a computer, software is always listening for requests from customers that visit your website. When someone clicks on a link in your website, a request is sent to your server and the web server software processes the request, handing it off to the various other systems on your computer, such as database and middleware, and sending the results back to the browser of the website visitor. In a sense, the web server acts as a *coordinator*, bringing together the various needed pieces into a single web page for your customer to see. The most popular web server software is Apache, an open source software system in use by millions of web servers.

- **Middleware**: For Magento installations, PHP is the middleware software that gives Magento and many other software systems their impressive power and capability. Many of the over 28,000 files that comprise a new Magento installation contain PHP code that builds the final web page dynamically. That is, each web page of a Magento store is actually built by combining several files according to the PHP code contained in each one. PHP code also sends queries (requests) to the database to retrieve, add, or delete store-related data such as customers, products, and categories.

- **Database**: A database is a repository of information, carefully structured to allow for fast retrieval and manipulation. Magento Community relies on **MySQL**, an open source database system now owned by Oracle, to store all its records. MySQL is a very popular, free database system (there are paid versions for very high-end requirements) used by everything from Magento to **WordPress**, as well as thousands of websites on the Internet. While not necessarily the fastest database platform on the market, as a free database system (and given its huge community of users and developers) it makes for a very capable Magento data source.

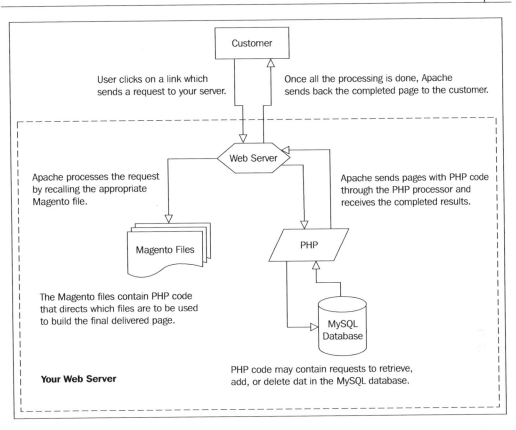

As the previous figure illustrates, web requests involve a complex interaction of the major server components to deliver an incredibly rich user experience. After over 15 years of developing web-based solutions, I'm still amazed at how quickly it all happens: click a link and in a matter of milliseconds, a web page begins to come into view in a browser!

Due to the complexity of the interaction, and the complexity of the Magento program structure (called architecture), your Magento store will better serve your customers if you take the extra time (and possibly added expense) of securing the right hosting environment.

Understanding types of hosting

Hosting plans range from a few dollars to hundreds of dollars per month, depending mainly on the type of server configuration you have. For most hosting providers, hosting is divided into three distinct categories:

- For small, startup Magento stores, a **shared server** is a great way to start. In essence, you are sharing the server with other hosting clients. However, expect to outgrow this if your store begins to handle more than about 5,000 visitors each day.

- A **Virtual Private Server**, or **VPS**, is not exactly a standalone machine. However, you are allocated dedicated resources, such as memory and CPU. This means that you have full use of these machine resources for your installation. The downside of a VPS, as with a shared server, is that other clients on the same server might compromise the availability of resources and throughput (bandwidth) for your own purposes.

- The most expensive solution is a **dedicated server**. As the name implies, you are renting a standalone computer server solely dedicated to your needs. No other clients are sharing your machine, so you will have full use of the resources of the machine. However, with most hosting providers, little (if any) support is provided to help you configure or troubleshoot the server. This is because dedicated server users are generally well versed in server configurations. In addition, having a dedicated machine means you could conceivably configure it in such a way that the hosting support team would not be able to understand or modify your settings.

Successful hosting guidelines

In my own evaluations of hosting providers for our Magento installations, I found out that prices and configurations varied quite widely. Through it all, though, I have been able to establish some basic guidelines you should consider when surveying possible hosting providers:

- If you've never managed a server, begin with a shared server plan. Choose a hosting provider that provides strong customer support and includes tools for handling your server configuration (such as **cPanel**, **DirectAdmin**, and **Plesk** web-based server management systems), and **phpMyAdmin**, a web-based tool for managing your MySQL database. Confirm with the hosting company whether they will help you upgrade to a VPS when necessary.

- If you plan on taking credit cards directly in your Magento store (beyond using **PayPal** or **Google Checkout**), you'll need to get an SSL Certificate (see the following information box) to protect your customer's information. Additionally, SSL encryption is used when your customer logs in to review their order history. Find out upfront what fees are charged for SSL Certificates, including installation. You can buy SSL Certificates elsewhere, but it usually incurs an installation fee by the hosting provider. The easiest way is to have the hosting provider order and install the SSL Certificate for you. A basic SSL Certificate runs as little as $15-25, although a fee of $50 (with installation included) is not uncommon. Avoid hosting providers that charge more than $50. The SSL charge is an annual fee.

Secure Socket Layer (SSL) Certificates

When you visit a website to shop, you may find that when the time comes to checkout, the URL in your browser changes from `http://www.domain.com` to `https://www.domain.com`. This means that any information you submit on a form is encrypted, or scrambled, before being sent to their web server. SSL encryption protects everything from credit card numbers to online banking transactions.

To achieve this security, the web server has two security keys, a private and public key. When you visit a secure web page, the public key is sent to your browser and is used to encrypt your data. When received by the web server, the private key is used to decrypt the data. Therefore, only data processed by a matching public and private key set can be read and processed by the server.

These keys are issued by means of an SSL Certificate, which is issued by one of a select few root certificate issuers. You can purchase SSL Certificates from a number of vendors, but they all get their certificates from the same issuers. To get an SSL Certificate, you have to provide business information and prove you own the domain you wish to secure. Furthermore, your hosting provider has to generate the private key to submit with the SSL Certificate application.

See the next section, *Avoiding the PCI headache*, for ways to avoid the need for securing an SSL Certificate. It's not difficult to obtain, but it is an annual fee that you may not need to incur.

- Ask about Magento experience. Any hosting provider can allow you to install Magento, but it pays (especially if you're new to Magento) to use a hosting provider that exhibits specific experience in hosting Magento sites. This will come in handy if you ever need assistance in troubleshooting your server configuration. Some hosting providers even provide "one-click" installers that alleviate the need to download Magento and upload it to your hosting server. In fact, we strongly encourage you to look for this feature, as it will allow you to skip most of the rest of this chapter!

- As with SSL Certificates, if you intend on taking credit cards using your own merchant account, you will at some point be scanned to check for PCI Compliance. **PCI (Payment Card Industry) Compliance** means that your server meets stringent criteria to protect cardholder information. Even if you don't store actual credit card information (and you shouldn't!), and if you allow customers to directly enter credit card information on your website, your server has to be impervious to hackers and other vulnerabilities that could expose the card information. Your hosting provider should configure their systems for PCI Compliance and agree to help you resolve any scans, which are conducted by your merchant account provider, that reveal any security vulnerabilities. See the next section for more information about PCI Compliance.

- Don't forget about backups, either. Make sure your hosting provider performs regular backups of their servers, at least on a daily basis. As dependable as servers generally are these days, a fatal crash is not impossible. What is their procedure for restoring crashed servers? What is their process for restoring your files and databases if you need to revert to a previous version?

Avoiding the PCI headache

To counter the continued threat of hackers stealing credit card and personal identity information from servers on the Internet, the credit card industry adopted a standard that every merchant is required to adhere to if they take credit card information online. If you intend on securing a merchant account to take major credit cards, you are required to be PCI Compliant in terms of how your online store is configured and operated.

As little as two years ago, small online retailers handling fewer than 10,000 transactions per year could simply answer a self questionnaire attesting that they did not store unencrypted credit card numbers on their servers or databases. For the vast majority of small business online retailers, this questionnaire was simple, and precluded the need to take extra steps to provide the highest level of server security.

That is no longer the case. All of our merchant clients are scanned quarterly by their merchant account providers to make sure that their web sites are without security vulnerabilities. In every case, these scans report one or more vulnerabilities which, when more fully evaluated, usually are *false positives*, meaning the vulnerabilities described don't actually exist or cannot be resolved based on the server operating system or software used, but don't present any real security threat.

Nevertheless, each scan must be analyzed and a response to every supposed vulnerability must be provided. This is taking more and more time from both our clients, ourselves as the designer of their store, and the hosting companies we use to actually host our clients' sites. Even hosting providers who are PCI Compliant will receive false positives that must be resolved. In short, PCI Compliance is becoming an increasing burden on merchants of all sizes.

There are ways you can manage your PCI Compliance, though, that will ease this burden:

- **Don't take credit cards on your website**. Instead of taking credit cards directly on your **Checkout** page in Magento, offer **PayPal Express** and/or Google Checkout to your customers (there are many others, especially for global businesses, such as **iDeal** and **CarteBlue**; Magento includes PayPal and Google Checkout functionality as part of its default installation). When they're ready to pay, they will be taken to the PayPal or Google servers to enter their payment information. Of course, this may not be preferred, as there is some drop-off from customers who are redirected to third-party payment providers, plus the fees charged by PayPal and Google may be more than you'd pay if you had your own merchant account. However, if you don't take payment information on your own server, you won't have PCI Compliance requirements.

- **Find a true PCI-compliant hosting provider**. Most hosting providers who cater to Magento installations have undergone the rigors of PCI Compliance. In most cases, you can provide a statement of PCI Compliance from the hosting provider to your merchant account provider that will satisfy their needs.

What about cloud servers?

The buzz today is **cloud computing**. However, for the purposes of running a Magento store, cloud computing is not ideal, for many significant reasons, not least of which is that the architecture of Magento does not lend itself well to being served on cloud servers due to the shared storage used in these configurations. Furthermore, since you are sharing resources with other users, you have almost no ability to tweak or fine-tune your server installation to maximize Magento performance.

I spent some time investigating the use of cloud servers for our Magento stores, consulting with some of the largest providers in the US. In each case, their recommendation is to avoid using cloud configurations for Magento. If you need more power and performance than a shared hosting account, opt for a virtual private server or lease an entire server for your own use.

For the purposes of our initial installation, we will use a basic hosting configuration. *Chapter 9, Optimizing Magento,* will help you enhance your configuration to handle higher load and visitor capacities.

I know you're wanting to ask, *but who do you use for hosting?* It's okay; given our experience with Magento, everyone asks us for a recommendation.

First, let me say there are several good companies that are fully capable of providing fast servers and who invest resources in knowing and supporting their Magento clients. You can find a list of companies who have taken steps to be an approved hosting partner with Magento at `http://www.magentocommerce.com/partners/find/hosting-partners/`.

For our clients, however, we use a company based in Pennsylvania called **MageMojo** (`www.magemojo.com`). MageMojo specializes only in Magento installations; they don't promote hosting any other solutions. In addition, their plans are a blend of a shared and virtual private server configuration: the benefits of a true, dedicated server at the cost of a shared server account. The servers also use solid-state hard drives which, in our experience, noticeably increase the speed of our Magento sites. Plus, each account comes with a one-year free SSL Certificate. MageMojo also handles all Magento installations, performance tuning, server management, and upgrades for you at no extra cost.

Keys to a successful installation

Magento has made the installation process a reasonably easy-to-follow affair. Since you've probably completed at least one installation before (and who hasn't tried Magento out-of-the-box?), you're familiar with the process.

However, you can make the installation more successful, just by adhering to the following battle-tested advice.

If you have never installed Magento before, it is not all that difficult. For assistance, there are a number of great resources, including the Packt book, *Magento: Beginner's Guide*. The Magento website also has an installation wiki (`http://www.magentocommerce.com/wiki/1_-_installation_and_configuration/magento_installation_guide`).

Avoiding the bleeding edge

If your Magento installation is to go "live" in quick order, you should always avoid installing the latest, greatest version of Magento (or any other platform, for that matter). As a practice, I never use any version where the third version number ends in zero, such as version 1.6.0 or 1.5.0. Although the platform or software creators have gone to great pains to debug the software before release, until a new version meets the challenges of the real world, you can count on a number of unforeseen bugs popping up. Avoiding "zeros" works with operating systems, software applications, and, yes, e-commerce systems.

However, if you are drooling over the new features of version Y.0, plan for installing version X.8 and upgrading to Y.1 when it is made available. Do a bit of research to find out what experiences people are having upgrading from X to Y, as well, so you'll be prepared.

As I write this book, Magento is at version 1.6.2.0, with version 1.7.x in beta stage. While these versions have added additional features to Magento, the basic architecture and operational features remain similar to 1.5.x. 1.5.x marked the start of a significant change in the Magento architecture, as compared to earlier versions.

Take your time

The complex power of Magento, which we cannot overstate, means that installing and configuring can be lengthy processes. You can't install Magento one day and be ready to sell tomorrow. Successful e-commerce involves a long list of to-do's, from payment methods, shipping methods, products, content, e-mail templates, forms, and much more. We will cover all important aspects in this book, which deserve your attention and consideration.

As far as the installation goes, the initial process is quite quick. You will be amazed that within 10 to 15 minutes you will actually have a functioning online store. Not one you would actually use as it is, of course, but one with which you can begin the magical transformation into a live, order-taking store.

Installing the sample data

When I first installed Magento years ago, I was eager to get a store up and running. I wasn't on a tight deadline (I'm foolish sometimes, but not reckless), but I was so convinced by what I had read that Magento was the answer, that I skipped a very important step—installing the sample data— and installed a bare basic version of Magento. Magento provides a configuration file that preloads products, websites, and stores to use with a new Magento installation.

When I viewed the installed store, it was, of course, empty. But not just of products; it had no content, no graphics, nothing. Barren! And so was the backend.

Back then, we had no Magento books, like this one, and the online documentation was sparse. I was lost. Without the sample websites and store views, I could not understand their relationships. I had little idea as to how the different product types were configured in the backend.

But, once installed, you cannot go back and install the sample data; it must be installed before installing Magento. After uninstalling and re-installing Magento (this time with the sample data), so much of Magento's power became clear.

While you may feel that spending time deleting the sample data is a worse prospect than not starting with it in the first place, it is not difficult to cleanse a Magento install of the sample data when you're ready to do so. It takes about five minutes or less, and the benefit you get from having the sample data installed greatly outweighs the inconvenience. I usually leave the sample data installed for quite some time, even as I begin configuring and adding the actual store information, as the data provides me with great reference examples.

 For more information on installing the sample data, see `http://www.magentocommerce.com/knowledge-base/entry/installing-the-sample-data-for-magento`.

Setting up Magento stores

As we discussed in *Chapter 1, Planning for Magento*, Magento leads the open source community in its ability to manage multiple websites and stores within a single installation. This power of Magento is often overlooked. It is also one of the more complex configuration issues.

Be forum vigilant

When researching how to configure multiple stores in Magento over the years, I have often consulted the discussion forums at the Magento website. With a user and developer base in the tens of thousands, the forums can be a lifesaver, as almost every possible challenge has been experienced and solved by others.

However, when you do find what appears to be a solution to an issue you may have with Magento, take care to confirm what versions of Magento it applies to. For example, configuring multiple stores in Magento changed radically between versions 1.3 and 1.4. Relative discussions in the forums were not always clear in terms of the version used, many times leading to testing solutions with painful (and sometimes unreconcilable) consequences.

Use the forums. They're a wonderful resource. Just remember to check for relevance to your installation!

To help illustrate how to configure multiple stores in Magento, let's set up an example. As shown in the following table, we are going to build two online businesses, each with their own categories and products, and each with two store views. The following table shows the **GWS (Global-Website-Store)** relationship of this example:

Business focus	Types of products	Domain	Language
Home products	Furniture	`acmefurniture.com`	English
Home products	Electronics	`acmeelectronics.com`	English
Outdoor products	Outdoor furniture	`acmeoutdoor.com`	English
Outdoor products	Outdoor furniture	`acmeoutdoor.com`	French

Planning your categories

Before creating your multiple stores, you need to plan your product category structure. In the Magento GWS hierarchy, websites are assigned to root categories. Root categories are not shown to your visitors, but rather are the top level under which all your subsequent categories reside.

Categories versus catalogs

There can be some confusion when using the terms categories and catalogs. This is due to the fact that Magento uses root categories as a synonym for catalogs. To keep this clear, a catalog is all the categories and products within one group, represented by the group's root category. Any level below the root category is what we will call categories throughout this book.

The following screenshot shows the category hierarchy of the sample data you may have installed during installation:

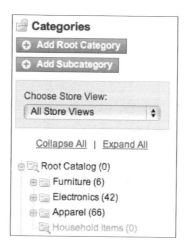

While Magento names the top sample data category, **Root Catalog,** you can use any name you wish. The categories, at the next level below the **Root Catalog,** are the top-level categories, which will usually appear on the navigation bar on the site.

To accomplish our example configuration, we need to create three root categories: **Furniture, Electronics,** and **Outdoor Furniture**. Once you create these under **Catalog | Manage Categories,** we would see the following categories (I have collapsed the sample data root category in the following screenshot; we will leave the sample data as we go through this example):

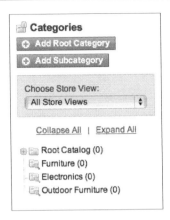

As you create categories, be sure to select **Yes** for the **Active** field.

If you want, you can add subcategories within these root categories, but for the purposes of creating multiple stores, it is not necessary at this point.

You may be asking, at this point, *Can multiple websites share the same root category?* The answer is yes. Due to the extensiveness of the GWS hierarchy, you can use the same product catalog for more than one business or website. For example, you might be creating multiple business entities, each selling the same products, but with separate payment gateways, store owners, and so on. While you can create duplicate catalogs with the same products, you can also use one catalog for both businesses. With GWS, you can control pricing, availability, and many other product attributes for each business. We'll be discussing categories and products in more detail in *Chapter 3, Managing Products*.

Disabling cache

While we will discuss caching more fully in *Chapter 9, Optimizing Magento*, as you build your stores, categories, CMS pages, and more, you should turn off the Magento cache so that your changes will appear immediately in your new store. In fact, anytime you are making changes to your Magento store, it's helpful to turn off the Magento cache.

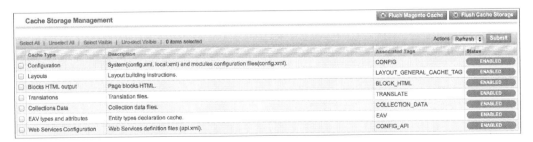

We can disable the Magento cache, using the following steps:

1. Go to **System | Cache Management**, in your Magento backend.
2. Click **Select All** in the left-most column of the table.
3. Select **Disable** in the **Actions** drop-down menu.
4. Click on the **Submit** button.

Setting up websites, stores, and store views

Next, let's go to **System | Manage Stores** in your Magento backend. You will see a screen with the sample data configuration, as shown in the following screenshot:

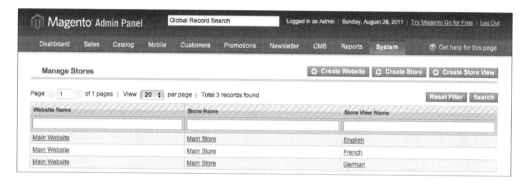

Without deleting these entries, let's create the websites we need for the example configuration:

1. Click on **Create Website**.
2. For **Name**, enter **Home Products**.
3. For **Code**, enter **home_products** (don't use spaces or capital letters).
4. Click on the **Save Website** button.
5. Repeat the steps, by clicking on **Create Website** again.
6. For **Name**, enter **Outdoor Products**.
7. For **Code**, enter **outdoor_products**.
8. Click on **Save Website**.

Your screen should look something like this:

Now, let's create the stores for our example:

1. Click on **Create Store**.

2. Leave **Home Products** as **Website** and enter **Furniture** for **Name**.

3. Select **Furniture** as **Root Category**.

4. Click on **Save Store**.

5. Click on **Create Store** again.

6. Leave **Home Products** as **Website** and enter **Electronics** for **Name**.

7. Select **Electronics** as **Root Category**.

8. Click on **Save Store**.

9. Once again, click on **Create Store**.

10. Select **Outdoor Products** for **Website**.

11. For **Name**, enter **Outdoor Furniture**.

12. Select **Outdoor Furniture** for **Root Category**.

13. Click on **Save Store**.

Now, let's stop a moment to review what we just did:

- We created two websites, one for each business (**Home Products** and **Outdoor Products**)

- Then, we created three stores (**Furniture**, **Electronics**, and **Outdoor Furniture**)

But wait! The example shows four stores; **Outdoor Furniture** is to have both an **English** language store and a **French** language store.

Since both the **English** and **French** stores will sell the same products, just in different languages (and, most likely, currencies), there really is only one **Outdoor Furniture** store. There will be, as we'll create next, two store views. This is where the store/store view nomenclature can get a bit confusing. Think of stores as analogous to different physical stores in different cities. Store views are different entrances into those stores. In our example, we have one store with different entrances for English-speaking and French-speaking customers.

At this point, our **Manage Stores** screen should look as follows:

Finally, we will create our necessary store views:

1. Click on the **Create Store View** button.
2. Leave **Electronics** as **Store**.
3. Enter **English** for **Name** (since you are not building different languages for this website, you could enter **Electronics**, or anything that helps define the store view for you).
4. For **Code**, enter **electronics_en** (the *_en* is used to denote English).
5. Change **Status** to **Enabled**.
6. Click on the **Save Store View** button.
7. Click on **Create Store View**.
8. Select **Furniture** for **Store**.
9. Enter **English** for **Name**.
10. Enter **furniture_en** for **Code**.
11. Change **Status** to **Enabled**.
12. Click on the **Save Store View** button.
13. Click on **Create Store View**.
14. Select **Outdoor Furniture** for **Store**.

15. Enter **English** for **Name**.

16. Enter **outdoor_en** for **Code**.

17. Change **Status** to **Enabled**.

18. Click on the **Save Store View** button.

19. Click on **Create Store View**.

20. Select **Outdoor Furniture** for **Store**.

21. Enter **French** for **Name**.

22. Enter **outdoor_fr** for **Code**.

23. Change **Status** to **Enabled**.

24. Click on **Save Store View**.

Now, your **Manage Stores** screen should look as follows:

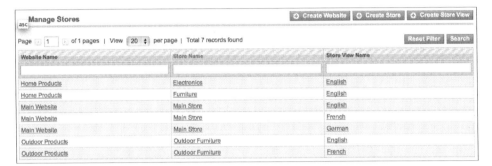

You have now created four new store views, for three stores of two websites.

Before these will be reachable by visitors, we have to undertake one additional bit of work. There are two ways in which Magento developers configure Magento to route multiple domain requests to the intended store views: modifying the .htaccess file and modifying the index.php file in the root Magento directory. I'll cover both methods, so please read over the next two sections before preceding to determine which is better for you.

Personally, I prefer modifying the .htaccess file instead of the index.php file. For one, updates to Magento that may modify the index.php file will not affect your configuration. For those of you who are not familiar with PHP programming language, modifying the .htaccess is also easier. That said, some developers prefer modifying the index.php, particularly if they have other modifications to make in the index.php file. To each his own: use the method with which you feel most comfortable.

Modifying the .htaccess file

The .htaccess file resides at the root of your Magento installation directory. This important file controls access to the directory, as well as setting certain parameters for handling the HTTP requests from visitors to your site.

For our purposes, we need to add additional code that will direct requests to the proper online store.

 Before editing the .htaccess file, it is always a good practice to make a copy as a backup in case you need to revert back to the original.

Open the .htaccess file in a text editor. We are going to add our needed code at the end of this file.

To assign domains to your different sites, the following template is used:

```
SetEnvIf Host www\.[domain] MAGE_RUN_CODE=[code]
SetEnvIf Host www\.[domain] MAGE_RUN_TYPE=[type]
SetEnvIf Host ^[domain] MAGE_RUN_CODE=[code]
SetEnvIf Host ^[domain] MAGE_RUN_CODE=[type]
```

This code instructs your web server to analyze an incoming URL based on the domain name, and inform Magento which website or store to deliver to the visitor:

- [domain] is your host domain, such as acmefurniture.com. By specifying both, with and without the www, we are accepting URL requests with or without the leading www.

- [code] is the code value you entered when you created the websites and store views in the previous process.

- [type] is the type of code you entered, either website or store (meaning store view).

Therefore, for our example configuration, we would add the following to our .htaccess file:

```
SetEnvIf Host www\.acmefurniture.com MAGE_RUN_CODE=furniture_en
SetEnvIf Host www\.acmefurniture.com MAGE_RUN_TYPE=store
SetEnvIf Host ^acmefurniture.com MAGE_RUN_CODE=furniture_en
SetEnvIf Host ^acmefurniture.com MAGE_RUN_TYPE =store
SetEnvIf Host www\.acmeelectronics.com MAGE_RUN_CODE=electronics_en
SetEnvIf Host www\.acmeelectronics.com MAGE_RUN_TYPE=store
SetEnvIf Host ^acmeelectronics.com MAGE_RUN_CODE=electronics_en
```

```
SetEnvIf Host ^acmeelectronics.com MAGE_RUN_TYPE =store
SetEnvIf Host www\.acmeoutdoor.com MAGE_RUN_CODE=outdoor_products
SetEnvIf Host www\.acmeoutdoor.com MAGE_RUN_TYPE=website
SetEnvIf Host ^acmeoutdoor.com MAGE_RUN_CODE=outdoor_products
SetEnvIf Host ^acmeoutdoor.com MAGE_RUN_TYPE=website
```

Naturally, you're wondering why the outdoor products site used a different configuration approach:

- If you are going to use one domain name for multiple store views, use website as the [type]. For our example, all visitors will go the www. acmeoutdoor.com, but will have the opportunity to switch from **English** to **French** using a drop-down menu in the header. In fact, by setting both languages with one domain, and a [type] of website, Magento will automatically add the language or store view to the drop-down menu selector:

- If, on the other hand, you have different URLs for each language (for example, www.acmeoutdoor.com and www.acmeoutdoor.fr), then you would add a .htaccess configuration for both, setting the [type] to store.

Temporary URLs

When you first install Magento, you may not be ready to point actual live domains to your new stores until you're ready. You can use this same configuration for other URL variations, such as teststore1.domain. com, teststore2.domain.com, and so on (subdomains of your actual domain). Or, be more descriptive: english.domain.com and french. domain.com. Later, when you're ready to go live, you can re-configure your .htaccess file to process the live domains.

Modifying the index.php file

As stated earlier, an alternative method to adding configurations to the .htaccess file is to modify code in the index.php file at the Magento root using a PHP case statement. The same principles, in terms of type (website or store), apply here, as well.

We can configure the index.php file, using the following steps:

1. Open the index.php file in the text editor of your choice.

2. In the code (the last line), find Mage::run($mageRunCode, $mageRunType).

3. Insert the necessary code right before this line.

The format for creating the PHP case statement is as follows:

```
switch($_SERVER['HTTP_HOST']) {
  case '[domain]':
  case 'www.[domain]':
    $mageRunCode = '[code]';
    $mageRunType = '[type]';
  break;
}
```

As with the .htaccess file, [code] refers to the website or store view code used when creating your websites and views, while [type] is either website or store. In our ongoing example, our index.php file would be modified as follows:

```
switch($_SERVER['HTTP_HOST']) {
  case 'acmefurniture.com':
  case 'www.acmefurniture.com':
    $mageRunCode = 'furniture_en';
    $mageRunType = 'store';
  break;
}
switch($_SERVER['HTTP_HOST']) {
  case 'acmeelectronics.com':
  case 'www.acmeelectronics.com':
    $mageRunCode = 'electronics_en';
    $mageRunType = 'store';
  break;
}
switch($_SERVER['HTTP_HOST']) {
  case 'acmeoutdoor.com':
  case 'www.acmeoutdoor.com':
    $mageRunCode = 'outdoor_products';
    $mageRunType = 'website';
  break;
}
```

Configuring Magento

Finally, we need to return to our Magento backend and tell Magento to use our domain names as Base URLs. **Base URLs** are what Magento uses to provide a complete URL path for the website pages it delivers to your visitors.

For example, if a visitor enters `http://acmefurniture.com` into their browser and arrives at your store, we can configure Magento to always convert that to the fuller `http://www.acmefurniture.com` for that request and all others afterwards. Additionally, we can set a different Base URL for secure SSL connections, such as `http://secure.acmestores.com`, in a case where we might be sharing an SSL Certificate among multiple stores, as we'll see in this section.

In our example, we are also creating two store views with different languages and, for our discussion, multiple currencies. Let's do it all now!

Configuring Base URLs

To begin, go to **System** | **Configuration** | **General** | **Web** in the Magento backend. At the upper-left of the screen is a drop-down menu labeled **Current Configuration Scope**. This determines at what level — **Global**, **Website**, or **Store View** — the configuration changes we make will have an effect. Everything we change at the **Global** level will affect all **Website** and **Store View** levels, unless we make another change at those levels: **Website** changes negate **Global** settings and **Store View** changes negate both **Global** and **Website** configurations. Not all settings can be changed at all levels. However, Magento notes to the right of each setting field the depth at which settings can be changed.

At this point, you should be at the **Global** level (**Current Configuration Scope** should be showing **Default Config**). There are two important global-level settings to consider, both under the **Url Options** (yes, for some reason, Magento spells URL as "Url") section in the center:

- **Add Store Code to Urls** is necessary if you are going to use a shared SSL or if you wish to use one URL for multiple store views, as in our multi-language example. By setting this to **Yes**, each URL adds the **Store View** code to the path, so that Magento will know for which store the request applies to. For example, for `acmeoutdoor.com`, requests for the English language site would look like `http://www.acmeoutdoor.com/outdoor_en/page.html`. Requests to the French language version would look something like `http://www.acmeoutdoor.com/outdoor_fr/page.html`. If you're using the same URL for more than one store view, set this value to **Yes**.

- **Auto-redirect to Base URL**, set to **Yes (302 Found)**, means that requests that come to the server in one manner, will be rewritten according to your preferred (or Base) URL. In our example, even though we are configured to process both `http://www.acmefurniture.com` and `http://acmefurniture.com`, we want all requests to be rewritten to the full www version. This helps us eliminate duplicate content from multiple URLs, which can penalize us with Google and other search engines. Without this rewrite, Google would consider requests for both URL versions to be duplicate copies of the same content. With this rewrite, there will only be one URL for any site content.

After setting these values, click **Save Config** and let's move on to setting the Base URLs.

1. Set the **Current Configuration Scope** to the store view you wish to edit. In our example, let's set it to **English** under **Furniture** (you'll notice that **Furniture** is dimmed in this menu; we can't really change the settings for a store, only a store view).

2. Open the section titled **Unsecure** in the center of the page.

3. For our **Furniture** store, enter **http://www.acmefurniture.com/** for **Base URL** (always include the trailing **/** at the end of URL).

4. Click on **Save Config**.

5. For our **Electronics** store, change the **Current Configuration Scope** to **English** under **Electronics**.

6. Once the page refreshes, enter **http://www.acmeelectronics.com/** for the **Base URL** in the **Unsecure** section.

7. Click on **Save Config**.

8. Since our outdoor sites are sharing the same URL, change the **Current Configuration Scope** to **Outdoor Products**, the **Website** scope level.

9. For the **Unsecure Base URL**, enter **http://www.acmeoutdoor.com/**.

10. Click on the **Save Config** button.

11. Go to **System | Cache Management** and click on **Flush Magento Cache**.

12. Go to **System | Index Management**. Click the checkbox to the left of **Catalog URL Rewrites**, then click on the **Submit** button in the upper-right. This will force Magento to rewrite all the catalog URLs according to your configuration.

Congratulations! You've now completed a process widely unknown and misunderstood in the Magento community. Yet, by understanding this process, you will find yourself swimming with ideas on how to leverage this power to create multiple sales channels, and ways of hosting multiple stores in a single Magento installation.

Using subdirectories for stores

If you want to use subdirectory paths in your store URLs, rather than the store code which may be less SEO friendly, you can create subdirectories in your root Magento directory for each store (for example, furniture, electronics, outdoor, great-furniture, cheap-electronics, outdoor-products, and so on) and place a copy of the index.php and .htaccess files in each directory. Instead of adding store codes to URLs, simply use the full directory path for the Base URLs. For example, if your subdirectory for furniture is /great-furniture, use http://www.acmefurniture.com/great-furniture/ for the Unsecure Base Url.

Using localization to sell globally

In our example configuration, we have set up one store with an English language store view and a French language store view. The standard installation of Magento Community only includes the English language for the United States. Therefore, to have the French language store display the content in French (or any other languages we desire), we have to install the language localization files for French. Furthermore, we can assign different currencies to each language site, so that visitors can view prices in the related currency.

Installing language files

The Magento community has created localization files for over 80 languages, translating as many as 15,000 words throughout the Magento files. Many languages remain incomplete, but the more popular languages, such as French, German, and Chinese are at or near 100 percent complete.

Follow these steps to install the localization files for a language:

1. Go to the **Translation** page at the Magento website (http://www.magentocommerce.com/translations).

2. Find the language you want to install and click **Select** on that row.

3. On the next page, click on **Package** to download the localization files for that language.

4. Unzip the downloaded file on your computer.

5. Upload the files to your site using your FTP client program, merging the files in the package with your installation.

6. If you're using a theme other than the default or Modern themes installed with Magento, you can find the folder within the downloaded package called `fr_FR`, located in the package at `app/design/frontend/default/default/locale/`. Copy this folder into your themes locale folder (for example, `app/design/frontend/[Package Name]/[Themeapp/design/frontend/default/[Theme Name]/locale/`).

> **Using Magento Connect to install language packs**
>
> In *Chapter 8, Extending Magento*, we cover installing third-party extensions using Magento Connect. You will find a great number of languages offered through Magento Connect (`http://www.magentocommerce.com/magento-connect`). These are installed just like extensions.

Once your language files are installed, we can assign the language to your store view (in this case, we will assign the French language store view for the sample data site):

1. In the Magento backend, go to **System | Configuration | General**.

2. Select **French** under **Main Store**, in the **Current Configuration Scope** drop-down menu.

3. In the center of the screen, click on **Locale Options**.

4. By default, the **Use Website** checkbox will be checked next to the **Locale** drop-down menu. Uncheck this box.

5. Select **French (France)** in the **Locale** drop-down menu.

6. Click on **Save Config**.

Now, when we go to our sample data store and select **French** from the drop-down at the top of the screen, much of the content on the site is in French, as shown in the following screenshot (of course, the images are not updated; you will have to create new images with translated copy):

You will also notice that there are many English labels, as well. Localization does not translate your content; it simply substitutes certain names and labels as configured in the `translate.csv` file you uploaded to your Magento installation.

Manually translating labels

So, how do you manually translate the remaining information? Let's take the category names as an example. In our sample data store, we see the three top level categories, **Furniture**, **Electronics**, and **Apparel**. For our French store, we'd like those translated to Meubles, L'électronique, and Habillement, respectively (I'm not fluent in French, so you might personally prefer different labels than these).

The first way to translate these categories is to change the actual name of the category in the **Manage Categories** area of the backend:

1. Go to **Catalog | Manage Categories**.

2. Select the appropriate store view (for example, **Main Store/French**) in the **Choose Store View** drop-down menu.

3. Select the category you wish to translate (for example, **Furniture**) in the category hierarchy.

4. Uncheck the **Use Default Value** checkbox to the right of the **Name** field.

5. Click on **Save Category** (for some reason, you may have to save the change to the checkbox before changing the **Name**; this may only be a temporary bug in Magento).

6. Enter the term you wish to display for the chosen store view (for example, **Meubles**).

7. Go to **System | Index Management** and re-index all shown indexes.

8. Click on **Save Category**.

Now, when we view the French language version of the sample data store, we see the renamed category in the top navigation bar, as shown in the following screenshot:

Switch back to **English**, and you'll once again see **Furniture** as the top category name. This method is useful for translating product names and page content, as well.

To change other labels on the site (if we don't like the terms used by the localization package, or there are other labels that need to be translated) we'll use the second method, called **inline translation**. For this example, we'll change the term **Checkout** in the French language sample data site to the possible French equivalent of Terminez L'achat (complete the purchase).

1. In the Magento backend, go to **System | Configuration | Developer**.

2. Select your desired **Store View** in the **Current Configuration Scope** drop-down menu (for example, **Main Store/French**).

3. Find the center section titled **Translate Inline**.

 Using inline translation means anyone visiting the page can change your titles. You should only use inline translation if your store is offline.

4. Deselect **Use Website** next to the **Enabled for Frontend** drop-down menu.

5. Select **Yes** in the drop-down.

6. Click on **Save Config** and refresh your Magento cache.

When you return to your storefront, you'll see small dotted borders around words that can be edited right on the page.

1. Roll your mouse over the word **Checkout** and click on the small book icon that appears just below the word. A pop-up will appear like the one shown as follows:

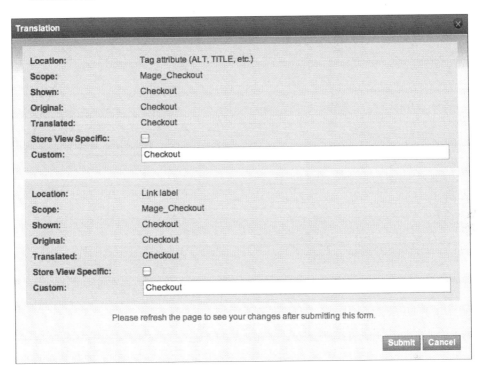

The top half of the screen allows you to change the tag attributes for the link, which is what will appear when the mouse hovers over the link.

The bottom part of this screen is what will actually appear on the screen.

2. Select both the checkboxes labeled as **Store Specific View**.

3. For both **Custom** fields, enter **Terminez L'achat**.

4. Click on the **Submit** button.

5. In the Magento backend, go to **System | Cache Management**. Regardless of what the pop-up screen says, you will usually need to flush Magento's cache in order to see your changes.

6. Click on **Flush Magento Cache**.

7. Return to your storefront and refresh your browser. Checkout has now been replaced by **Terminez L'achat**.

 Use *Ctrl + F5* (Windows) or *Command + R* (Mac) to easily refresh your browser window.

Remember to return to **System | Configuration | Developer** and turn off **Translate Inline** when you're finished.

Converting currencies

To continue our French set up, we want to show prices in euros. Again, Magento provides multiple means of accomplishing this.

The process of configuring your installation to handle multiple currencies follows this flow:

1. Establish your base currency, and its scope. You can have different base currencies for each website within your installation (but not store view).

2. Select the additional currencies in which your site will be available: what currencies will you be using in your stores?

3. Designate the default displayed currencies for specific stores.

4. Configure automatic currency conversions, if so desired, or manually adjust prices for any additional currencies.

It begins with the base currency

The **base currency** is the currency in which you operate your business. If you're a US business, you most likely operate in dollars. That means your transactions with payment gateways and shipping calculations are in dollars. Any automatic currency conversions you establish will be based on US dollars. Likewise, if your base currency is euros, all your monetary calculations will be based on euros, even if you choose to display prices to your visitors in pounds sterling or Fijian dollars.

To begin, let's assume that the US dollar will be our base currency, but we will be allowing both dollars and euros to be used on our French language store:

1. Go to **System | Configuration | Catalog**.

2. Select **Default Config** for **Current Configuration Scope**.

3. Click on the center section titled **Price**.

4. Change **Catalog Price Scope** to **Website**.

5. Click on **Save Config**.

We have now allowed the ability to adjust our available currencies at the **Website** level, rather than the overall **Global** level. If you know that your base currency will always be the same throughout your installation, you can leave this set to **Global**.

1. Go to **System | Configuration | Currency Setup**.

2. Select all the various currencies you would like to have allowed in the stores within our installation, as a default, in the **Allowed Currencies** selection field. For our purposes in this example, we only want **US Dollar** selected.

3. Change the **Base Currency** and **Default Display Currency** to reflect your preferred choices. For our example, we will leave them as they are: **US Dollar**.

The allowed currencies are set up under **System | Configuration | System** in the center section titled **Currency**. By default, Magento preselects all current currencies. The others are obsolete currencies, but available to you should you find a need to display prices in these currencies.

Next, we need to change the default currency of the **French** language store:

1. Go to **System | Configuration | Currency Setup**.

2. Select **Main Store/French** in the **Current Configuration Scope** drop-down menu.

3. In the center section, select **British Pound Sterling**, **Euro**, **Japanese Yen**, and **US Dollar** in the **Allowed Currencies** selection field (we're adding a couple of extra ones for illustrative purposes).

4. Choose **Euro** in the **Default Display Currency** drop-down menu.

5   Click on **Save Config**.

Of course, we know that dollars do not convert to euros on a one to one basis (it's possible, but highly unlikely).

Let Magento automatically convert currencies

Now, if that little piece of the process didn't impress you with the depth of its flexibility, the following should: automated currency conversions.

A feature of Magento is its ability to automatically and periodically set a conversion rate between currencies that will be used to calculate prices at various allowed currencies. Magento calls upon a third-party service called **Webservicex** to provide the conversion rates.

To set up periodic currency conversions, follow these steps:

1. Go to **System | Configuration | Currency Setup**.
2. Select **Default Config** in the **Current Configuration Scope** drop-down menu.
3. Click on **Schedule Import Settings** to open the center section.
4. Change **Enabled** to **Yes**.
5. Select a **Start Time** (most likely, you would want a time late at night or early in the morning to prevent prices from changing during your busiest shopping periods; it might surprise some shoppers!).
6. Select a **Frequency**. **Daily** is fine, but if you want less frequent updates, choose **Weekly** or **Monthly**.
7. Enter an e-mail address for whomever would like to receive any e-mail alerts if the currency conversion update fails.
8. Click on **Save Config**.

Next, let's set the initial conversion rates:

1. Go to **System | Manage Currency Rates**.
2. The first record on this screen is labeled **USD** on the left. The remaining fields, one for each allowed currency, are blank.
3. To initiate the first currency conversion update, click on **Import**.
4. Now the fields are filled, displaying the rate at which one US dollar converts.
5. Before these can take effect, though, click on **Save Currency Rates**.

Based on your settings for the automatic updates, these figures will change every day, week, or month. After manually updating currency rates, flush your Magento cache.

Let's take a look at what we accomplished. Go to the sample data frontend site in English and using the category navigation at the top, go to the **Furniture | Living Room** category. The top-left quadrant of the page should look as follows:

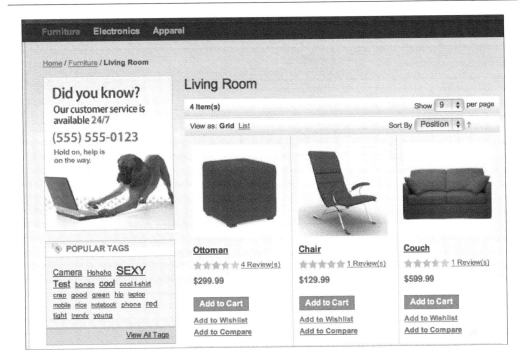

Change the language of the site to **French**, and observe the difference in the page:

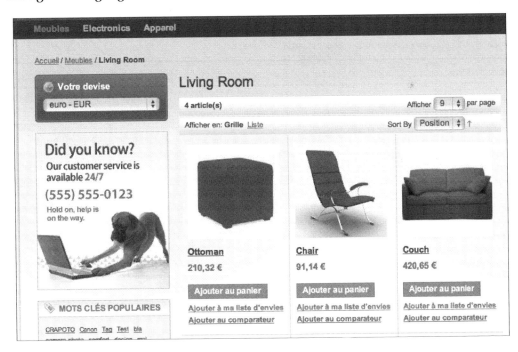

As you can see, in the French site, there is an added currency selector at the top of the left column and the product prices are shown in euros, rather than dollars. Since we configured the system to allow more than one currency in the French site, the currency selector automatically appears and will display all allowed currencies (euros and dollars).

Strategies for backups and security

If you're a seasoned developer or webmaster, you certainly have protocols in place for protecting your work, from daily backups to failover servers. If you are a designer or site administrator, your backups are managed by your hosting provider or system administrator; you probably don't think much about backups on a daily basis.

However, with any complex configuration, a failure or mistake can still lead to hours and hours of lost time. Daily system backups are only good for what was done up to the time the backup was made. If you've worked with me in these first two chapters, you've already made a significant number of changes and configurations that, if you had to go back to yesterday's system backup, could take you hours to re-create.

I'm a retentive guy. I like to have backups, backups, and more backups, all along the way. Without interfering with how your systems are backed up, allow me to suggest some hard-learned strategies for working with Magento.

Backend backups

Under **System | Tools | Backups**, you can create backups of your Magento database with a simple click. You should make a backup before and after doing any significant changes or configurations to your installation. It's simple and, until you get lots of product and customer data, it's fairly quick. These backups cannot be automated; these are not system backups. These backups should be considered more like bookmarks, dumps of your Magento database captured at a particular point in time that will allow you to go back in time to an earlier set of data.

Unfortunately, these backups are not as easily restored. The file created is a SQL statement file dump of your database that is stored on your server under var/ backups in your root directory. You can download this file, import it into **phpAdmin** or another MySQL client tool, and run to rebuild your database as before.

File structure backups

What about your actual Magento files on the server? Again, your system backups should prevent any major loss on this front. However, I make it a general practice to download the full installation onto my computer using an FTP client. Periodically, I use an FTP program to synchronize or merge the online store files with my local files, so I'm up to date with what is on the server.

> A more secure method of uploading and downloading files to a server is to use **SFTP (Secure File Transfer Protocol)**, a common method allowed by almost all hosting providers.

The reason I do this is that if I want to make changes in the code files, a theme's CSS file, or edit an image, I first make a duplicate of my copy of the original server file. Then, I make the changes I want to make to the original copy and upload it to the server. If I have somehow made a fatal error and need to recover quickly, I can simply copy the contents of the duplicate copy I made earlier, paste it into the original copy, and upload it again to the server, and I'm back in business.

Keeping it secure

I haven't heard of anyone hacking into a Magento configuration. While it's possible to hack anything, Magento is a pretty solid piece of work. As with system backups, those responsible for your servers are most likely taking steps to prevent physical access to your hard drive and files.

> Although I feel safe using Magento for an e-commerce platform, you should note that not all third-party extensions necessarily provide the same level of secure programming techniques. While I have not experienced problems before, I do make it a habit to only use extensions that have been downloaded by a large number of Magento users, and have been commented on by users who have had ample opportunity to use (and break) the extension. I also have a test Magento installation on which I first install extensions to test before deploying to a client installation.

I am most concerned with in terms of my work as a Magento
is that of user access. Under **System | Permissions**, you can set up
users. Generally, I establish the following roles:

Sales, with access to orders, promotions, and customers

- Product management, with access to catalogs and products

- Marketing, with access to customers, CMS, promotions, newsletters, and reports

- Management, with access to everything other than the system configuration tools

And as for me, the administrator, I usually create another user in my organization with full privileges should I be on vacation or sick.

The one caveat about users and roles which you should be aware of is that Magento does not allow you to assign permissions based on website or store view. Unfortunately, a user with sales access has permission to view all orders and all customers. Hopefully, this will be improved upon in future Magento releases.

Summary

Boy, we covered a lot in this chapter! Yet, despite all the screen captures and instructions, you most likely found the configuration processes not as daunting as first imagined. The sophistication of Magento requires a certain degree of complexity.

In this chapter, we:

- Implemented our planned multi-store configuration

- Learned how to configure our stores for multiple languages and currencies

- Covered some basic practices to ensure that our work survives data loss

Next, we begin the process of creating our category and product infrastructure. After all, the reason we're here is to sell products!

3
Managing Products

After successfully installing Magento, you can now take on the task of creating and configuring your store. You could begin crafting the design that reflects your store's brand, or you could start configuring the many settings that will direct how your customers will interact with your online store.

However, selling online really boils down to the products that you're selling. Additionally, many of Magento's configurations depend on the products that you're offering and how they are arranged into categories.

Therefore, when I create a new Magento-powered store, I begin at the "root," so to speak: the products.

In this chapter, we will tackle the following:

- Creating catalogs and categories
- Adding products manually and importing en masse
- Setting up reviews, tags, and feeds that help promote your products

Catalogs and categories

The use of the terms "catalogs" and "categories" in Magento can be a bit confusing, as Magento tends to use these terms with some inconsistency. Let us define these according to our purposes.

Understanding catalogs

In *Chapter 2, Successful Magento Installation*, I created two new web sites, three new stores, and four store views. Each store was assigned to a root category which we created under **Catalogs | Manage Categories** in the Magento backend.

I consider each root category as a catalog, a collection of products to be sold within a given Magento store. In my example, as illustrated in the next diagram, we have three stores, each with its own catalog: selling electronics, furniture, and outdoor furniture. Each catalog will have its own hierarchy of categories and its own selection of products.

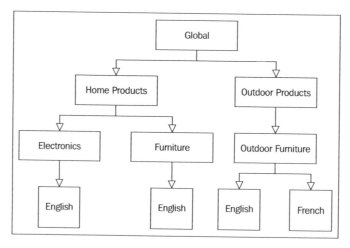

What if you have products that belong in all Catalogs, such as—to continue our example—wall clocks? No worries. With Magento, you can assign the same product to more than one catalog, and, as you'll see later in this chapter, to more than one category within a catalog.

I like to think of a catalog as just that: A catalog much like you used to get from *Sears Roebuck* in days gone by. When I was a kid, every year we received the huge *Sears Roebuck* catalog in the mail, free of charge. You could also request more specific catalogs, such as appliances or tools. These "specialty" catalogs contained many of the same products found in the main catalog, but also had other products not found in the main catalog. With Magento, we could create the same catalog assortment as Sears produced, only online.

Understanding categories

With catalogs now defined, limiting categories to the subdivision within a catalog is more succinct. This distinction is important though, because if you've had a chance to look around your new Magento installation—and provided you installed the sample data—you'll see that while the top navigation menu in the Admin backend is labeled **Catalogs**, you actually create "root categories" to represent individual catalogs. Magento goes further in this vein of confusion by calling the top, sample root category, "Root Catalog".

To help illustrate how we can use a common language to plan our product classifications, let's use the following outline for planning the three example catalogs that we described earlier. Catalogs are in **bold**, while categories are indented:

- **Electronics**
  - Personal
  - Home Entertainment
  - Computers
  - Accessories

- **Furniture**
  - Living
  - Dining
  - Bedroom
  - Accessories

While there are similarly named categories among the catalogs, each would contain only those products relevant to the purpose of the catalog. As mentioned before, you will still be able to assign products to more than one catalog, as well as to more than one category within a catalog.

Special categories

Magento provides some inherent tools used while grouping products for special display purposes. For example, by designating **New From** and **New To** dates in a **Product Detail** screen, as shown in the next screenshot, Magento will display a product within a **New Products** block if today's date falls within the range of these dates:

However, in some cases, you may want to display groups of products for other reasons. It's not uncommon to show "Featured" products on an e-commerce website. You may even want to show products grouped by family or purpose.

Let's take the case of creating a "Featured" products section for our home page. Let's also assume that you don't want "Featured" as a category in your navigation bar, just as a "special" Category.

1. Go to **Catalog | Manage Categories** in your Magento backend.

2. Click on the root category under which you wish to create your special category.

3. Click on **Add Subcategory**.

4. In the central part of the screen, enter the following values:
   ○ **Name**: *Featured*
   ○ **Is Active**: *Yes*
   ○ **Include in Navigation Menu**: *No*

5. Click on the tab at the top labeled **Category Products**.

6. Find the product that you wish to add to this category and check the box in the left-most column.

7. Click on **Save Category**.

8. After the screen refreshes, note the **ID** number of the category at the top of the screen, as shown in the following screenshot (in this example, the category **ID** is "53"):

You've now created a new category called **Featured** and added some products. We now need to add a block to the home page that will display your featured products.

9. Go to **CMS | Pages**.

10. Click on the **Home** page for the store that you wish to update.

11. Click on the side tab labeled **Content**.

12. If the WYSIWYG editor is showing, click on **Show / Hide Editor** to reveal the HTML code.

13. In the code, find where you want to put your **Featured Products** section, and insert the following:

```
{{block
  type="catalog/product_list"
  category_id="53"
  template="catalog/product/list.phtml"}}
```

14. You may want to add a title before this, such as the following:

```
<h3>Featured Products</h3>
```

15. Click on **Save Page** (or **Save and Continue Edit**).

    When you view the home page, you should see a section displaying the featured items you assigned to this special category:

Furthermore, you can access this category and its products by appending the name of the special category to your store URL. For example, to see the entire **Featured Products** category, you can go to http://www.yourstoredomain. com/featured.html.

In *Chapter 6, Managing Non-Product Content*, we'll go into more detail about blocks and how to use them in creative ways, giving your online store more features and functionality.

Managing products the customer-focused way

The heart of any online store is the selection of products offered to visiting customers. Yet, as simple as that may sound, creating online stores to present the vast array of products and product types has proven to be one of the most challenging quests for platform programmers.

If all stores sold each product as an individual item without different colors, sizes, or add-ons, e-commerce would be much simpler. But, that's not how the real world works. If you sell T-shirts (the classic example for this discussion), you might sell each color as a separate item, especially if you only offer a few shirts. However, it would make shopping very cumbersome for your customers if you also had each size of each color listed as a separate product.

People shop by product style, then decide upon variations, such as size and color. To reflect this shopping "workflow," we need to create products in our store that are presented in the most convenient and logical manner possible.

Types of products

To accommodate the many different types of products that can be sold online, Magento groups products into five types, listed next.

Simple products

Simple products are those which are sold individually. For example, if you're selling watches, you may offer different types of bands for each watch; but in general, the product is sold as an individual unit.

Complex products

In Magento, a complex product refers to a product that has to be configured differently, as it generally relies on other products in your store, or is not a physical product. To clarify, let's explore each type of complex product.

Grouped products

A grouped product is one that displays several similar products on a single product page. Shoppers can buy only those items in the group that they wish to add individually. Grouping products is a wonderful way to display coordinated items.

The sample data that you installed includes a grouped product for a furniture set, shown as follows:

Configurable products

Some products are offered with variants, such as colors and sizes. If the product variants do not require separate **SKUs (Stocking-keeping units)**, you could use a simple product type, with an option to select a size. However, in most cases, each variant of a product requires a different SKU. Many also are priced differently. For example, if you're selling a basketball shoe, it might be one price for sizes 5-12, but cost an additional $15 for sizes 13 and above. To track inventory for each size, each individual product SKU needs to be entered as a separate simple product. But, you don't want to show 12 listings of the same shoe, one for each size; that would be cumbersome for your online customers.

With configurable products, you can create each individual SKU as a simple product, but show them all as one product with variants. You can even have more than one variant. Your basketball shoe might come in different sizes and colors.

The next screenshot shows a configurable product included in the sample data. Notice the **Size** drop-down menu and how the price changes for each variant included.

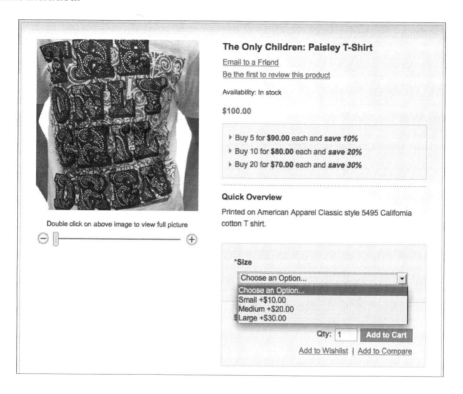

Configurable products are one of the most powerful product features of Magento. I am finding more and more ways to use this to better present products for our clients, as I'm sure you will, too.

Virtual products

Products that don't require inventory or shipping, such as warranties or services, are called virtual products. As you'll see later in this chapter, the creation of a virtual product is very similar to creating a simple product.

Bundle products

Bundle products are perhaps one of the most interesting product types in Magento because their application as a product allows you to offer some amazing customization capabilities to your customers.

The classic example of a bundle product is that of the "Build-Your-Own" computer, as shown on the following page. By bundling many different products together, you can give your customers the ability to create their desired product simply by choosing from an array of possible choices.

Amazingly, Magento handles all the pricing—including the **From** and **To** price range shown—automatically from the products you add into the bundle.

Downloadable products

Products that are distributed electronically, such as eBooks, music files, or computer programs, are configured in Magento as downloadable products. By using this product type, Magento helps you manage how the products are distributed and the number of times they can be downloaded.

Attributes and attribute sets

Before we can begin adding products, we have to learn about one very important aspect of Magento product management: attributes. Once you understand how attributes are used in creating and managing products you may, as I did, find new and creative ways to use attributes for your own store websites.

Product attributes

Every product in Magento contains a number of fields, such as price, SKU, name, and so on. Each of these can be considered as attributes of a product. Attributes, in essence, serve to describe the different features of a product.

Magento gives you the ability to alter some default attributes. More importantly, you can create new attributes that will help you provide better information to your customers. For example, if you sell furniture, you may want a field to describe the wood finish or upholstery cloth. Certain attributes can be used in the layered navigation or as comparison fields when comparing different products.

Attributes are added to attribute sets (see the next section) so that they will be included as part of the **Product** edit screen. If you want to enter sizes when creating products, for example, you'll need to have an attribute for this as part of the **Product** edit screen.

As shown in the next screenshot, this partial list of attributes, in part created from the sample data, shows a variety of different possible product features.

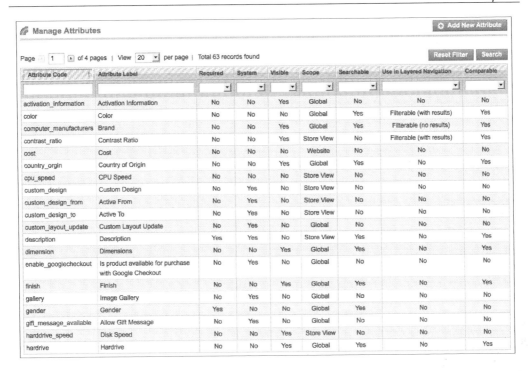

Attribute Code	Attribute Label	Required	System	Visible	Scope	Searchable	Use in Layered Navigation	Comparable
activation_information	Activation Information	No	No	Yes	Global	No	No	No
color	Color	No	No	No	Global	Yes	Filterable (with results)	Yes
computer_manufacturers	Brand	No	No	Yes	Global	Yes	Filterable (no results)	Yes
contrast_ratio	Contrast Ratio	No	No	Yes	Store View	No	Filterable (with results)	Yes
cost	Cost	No	No	No	Website	No	No	No
country_orgin	Country of Origin	No	No	Yes	Global	Yes	No	Yes
cpu_speed	CPU Speed	No	No	No	Store View	No	No	No
custom_design	Custom Design	No	Yes	No	Store View	No	No	No
custom_design_from	Active From	No	Yes	No	Store View	No	No	No
custom_design_to	Active To	No	Yes	No	Store View	No	No	No
custom_layout_update	Custom Layout Update	No	Yes	No	Global	No	No	No
description	Description	Yes	Yes	No	Store View	Yes	No	Yes
dimension	Dimensions	No	No	Yes	Global	Yes	No	Yes
enable_googlecheckout	Is product available for purchase with Google Checkout	No	Yes	No	Global	No	No	No
finish	Finish	No	No	Yes	Global	Yes	No	Yes
gallery	Image Gallery	No	Yes	No	Global	No	No	No
gender	Gender	Yes	No	No	Global	Yes	No	No
gift_message_available	Allow Gift Message	No	Yes	No	Global	No	No	No
harddrive_speed	Disk Speed	No	No	Yes	Store View	No	No	No
hardrive	Hardrive	No	No	Yes	Global	Yes	No	Yes

Let's go over the various fields available when creating a new attribute. To begin, go to **Catalog | Attributes | Manage Attributes** in your backend. You should see a screen similar to the previous screenshot.

As an example, let's create a new attribute that we will use for our tennis wear to show the type of material used in our garments. As we go through this process, you'll get a better understanding of how attributes are created and the choices that you have to make while creating a new attribute. If you want to create our example attribute, enter the values shown in brackets ([ ]) after each field description.

Click on **Add New Attribute** at the upper right-hand side of your screen. If you look at the left sidebar, you'll see two tabs, **Properties** and **Manage Label / Options**. This means that this screen is actually two screens.

On the **Properties** screen:

- **Attribute Code**: This is a unique value used by Magento in linking data together. Therefore, you can use any word or phrase, but substitute any spaces with underscores or hyphens. [Enter *garment_material*]

- **Scope**: This can be a bit confusing, so allow me to clarify how **scope** is used here. Think about how the attribute will be used for a product. In our example, the material of a garment will be the same at all scope levels. That is, we're unlikely to choose *cotton* for one store and *polyester* for another, for the same garment. Therefore, we would choose a **Global** scope. On the other hand, if you might offer a product in *red* in one store, but *green* in another, then the scope would be **Website** or **Store View**, depending on how you structure your stores. [*Global*]

- **Catalog Input Type for Store Owner**: In case you didn't already know—you're the Store Owner—the person who enters data into Magento, regardless of whether you actually own the store or not (you'll see this term used in various places throughout Magento). In this field, you will decide what type of entry can be made when the attribute is given a value. Each entry type has different consequences for how the attribute can be used. [*Dropdown*].

  ○ **Text Field**: A blank field in which you can enter whatever value you wish. This is useful for entering values such as voltage, length, or CPU speed. Values are limited to 255 characters.

  ○ **Text Area**: A larger blank field for data entry. You could use this field type for entering installation instructions or a list of minimum requirements.

  ○ **Date**: A date entry could be used to denote some future or past date, such as release date for a downloadable book.

  ○ **Yes/No**: If your attribute value, such as "Hardcover Available", can be answered as Yes or No.

  ○ **Multiple Select**: If you want to provide a set list of values for an attribute, but be able to select more than one for a given product, use a Multiple Select entry type. For example, you may want a list of available cloth types for your tennis wear. A garment might be available or may contain more than one cloth type. Therefore, with a Multiple Select field, you can select all the applicable types.

  ○ **Dropdown**: Basically, a Dropdown is the same as a Multiple Select, but you can only select one of the listed values.

  ○ **Price**: A new attribute using a Price field lets you create an alternative pricing option for a product. As we'll see later when we create products, Magento provides fairly extensive pricing options, such as Special Price, Tier Price, and Cost. However, you may want to include additional price values, such as Wholesale Cost and Distributor Cost for internal use.

- ○ **Media Image**: This field type allows you to upload an image that could be used on the product's description page. You could use this to show a schematic or a brand logo for a product.

- ○ **Fixed Product Tax**: Some governments impose fixed taxes, such as a VAT (value added tax), on certain goods. You could use a Fixed Product Tax type for entering this value for a product. This tax would be added to each purchase.

- **Default Value**: For appropriate field types, you can enter a default value that will appear whenever you create a new product that uses this attribute (not applicable for the Dropdown input type).

- **Unique Value**: If each product using this attribute is to have a unique value, set this to *Yes*. For example, a field for UPC code would be unique, as no two products can have the same UPC code. [*No*]

- **Values Required**: Set this to *Yes* if you want to force a value to be entered or selected for a product. [*No*]

- **Input Validation for Store Owner**: You can test the value entered to make sure that it conforms to certain criteria: *Decimal Number, Integer Number, Email, URL, Letters,* or *Letters and Numbers*. A UPC code, for example, would be an *Integer Number* (no decimals). [*Not applicable*]

- **Apply To**: Certain attributes may only be applicable certain product types. For example, an attribute for Assembly Time might only apply to Bundle products. [*All Product Types*]

- **Use To Create Configurable Products**: We'll learn more about configurable products later in this chapter when we create a configurable product, which will make this field more relevant. [*No*]

- **Use in Quick Search**: In Magento, a "Quick Search" is performed using the single search field shown on every page, such as the one in the next screenshot. When searching for a match, this attribute, if this value is *Yes*, will be used as a search matching value. [*Yes*]

- **Use in Advanced Search**: One of the default pages in Magento is an Advanced Search. If you set this field to *Yes*, this attribute will be added to the list of possible search criteria on the **Advanced Search** page. The next screenshot shows an **Advanced Search** page from the sample data store. [*Yes*]

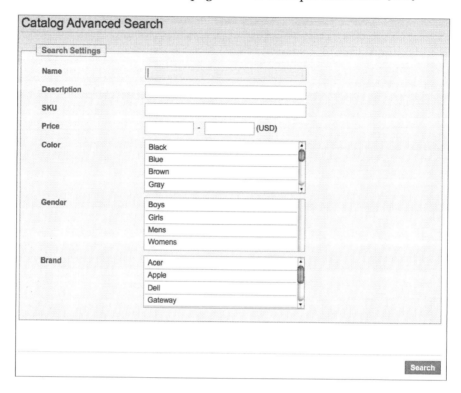

- **Comparable on Front-end**: Magento includes the ability for customers to select two or more products and show them in a pop-up window in a comparison table. This allows customers to compare attributes across the selected products. If you want this attribute to be included in this comparison chart, choose *Yes*. [*Yes*]

- **Use in Layered Navigation**: The use of attributes in layered navigation can be a powerful shopping tool for your customers. Since Magento needs to set values in order to construct the layered navigation criteria, only the *Dropdown*, *Multiple Select*, and *Price* field types can be used in layered navigation. *Filterable (with results)* means that this attribute will only appear in layered navigation if there are actual products with attribute values matching one of the values in this attribute. *Filterable (without results)* will show this attribute in layered navigation at all times. [*Filterable (with results)*]

- **Use in Search Results Layered Navigation**: When customers do a product search on your site, the results include a layered navigation sidebar. As with the previous field, only the *Dropdown*, *Multiple Select*, and *Price* field types can be used. [*Yes*]

- **Use for Promo Codes**: As we'll cover in *Chapter 5, Configuring to Sell*, promotional codes can be used to provide discounts to customers. These codes are established using rules, such as "price over $100" or "shipping weight under 100 pounds". You could use an attribute to create promotions, such as "green colored garments" (to promote St. Patrick's Day) or "XXL sizes" (to move an overstocked inventory of large shirts). [*No*]

- **Position**: If you want to manipulate the order in which layered navigation attributes are listed, you can use this field, entering numbers in ascending order for top-to-bottom positions. [*Leave blank*]

- **Allow HTML Tags on Frontend**: When entering text values, you may want to include HTML tags, such as `<strong>` for bold or `<i>` for italics. Magento, by default, filters these out to avoid the possibility of breaking your design. You can, however, allow HTML tags if you feel it necessary to use them in presenting an attributes, content. For example, you may want to be able to enter CPU speeds with "MHz" in italics for added emphasis. [Not applicable]

- **Visible on Product View Page on Front-end**: In most product detail page designs, there will be a section called "Additional Information". This section contains a table listing all attributes for the product in which this field is set to *Yes*. [*Yes*]

- **Used in Product Listing**: If *Yes*, this attribute will always be shown in a search results list, if your design is modified to show this attribute. I've found that most designs do not automatically add new attributes with this field set to *Yes*. [*No*]

- **Used in Sorting in Product Listing**: Earlier, we talked about changing the default sorting for a category, such as by *Best Value*, *Name*, or *Price*. By setting this field to *Yes*, you will create a new sorting criteria for lists that include products with this attribute. For example, you could add "CPU Speed" as a sorting criteria for computer products. [*No*]

Before you can save your new attribute, you still need to add at least one more piece of data. Click on the left sidebar menu called **Manage Label / Options**.

For your attribute to be understood on the frontend, you need to provide a title, such as *Garment Material*. This value should be entered into the first space labeled **Admin**.

If you want the title to be different for your stores, enter the other values in the spaces shown. Any spaces left blank will automatically use the **Admin** value.

When you create an attribute with multiple selections, such as with our garment material example, an additional table called **Manage Options** will be visible, such as the one shown in the next screenshot. This chart is used to list the possible choices that you will use for this attribute when you create or edit a product.

To add a choice, click on **Add Option** and fill in the information, using the same process you did for the title. You can add as many options as you like. For our garment material, let's add **Cotton**, **Polyester**, and **Blend** in the **Admin** column, as shown in the next screenshot. In order that Magento list these in this particular order, enter **10** for Cotton, **20** for Polyester, and **30** for Blend in the **Position** column. Click on **Save Attribute** to save this example attribute, which we will be using in the next section.

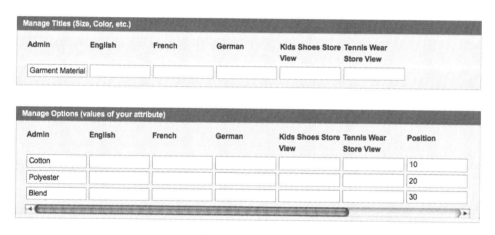

After creating a new attribute, you may see a notice at the top of your screen that one or more of Magento's indexes need updating. Click on the link shown and re-index any index with a **REINDEX REQUIRED** message showing in the **Status** column.

Attribute sets

If you thought creating attributes was interesting (you have to admit that Magento attributes offer tremendous flexibility and power to your product management), hold on to your seat!

Before you can use attributes, you have to assign them to attribute sets. Each product that you create is first assigned to a set of related attributes for you to use. So, before you set out to add products to Magento, let's discuss some general concepts for using attribute sets:

- If you have a wide variety of product types (such as clothing, computers, shoes, and so on), consider creating attribute sets for each type, particularly if each product type will have different attributes. "Size" may be important for shoes, but not for computers. Alternatively, computers may include "voltage", which is not applicable to shoes. When segregating your attributes by product type, you will have better control over the attributes for each product. Additionally, any attributes for which **Visible on Product View Page on Front-end** is set to *Yes* will appear on the product detail page regardless of whether a value is provided or not. You don't want a shoe to show a N/A value for voltage; it might confuse your buyers ("Do your shoes have voltage?").

- If you have to import large quantities of products, assigning each to a different attribute set can be quite tedious and time-consuming. In this case, it may be wiser to create one attribute set for all products being imported, but make sure that attributes in the set are:

  - Not required for entry

  - Fairly generic (for example, "Power requirements" instead of "voltage", "watts", and "amps", separately)

I often have to import 20-30,000 products at a time; assigning different attribute sets for each product type would be too expensive in terms of time spent.

> One challenge with attribute sets is that once assigned to a product, you cannot re-assign the product to another attribute set. However, you can modify an attribute set, which will also update a product's attributes. Therefore, take some time to experiment with different attribute sets and add new products. View the results in your frontend to see how they appear to your customers. Before you get too far down the road in adding new products, it's best to get a firm handle on how attributes work and how they affect your stores. I can tell you from experience, it's no fun having to delete and re-add hundreds of products because you suddenly decide to assign the products to a new attribute set.

Creating an attribute set

To continue our example, let's create a new attribute set for our tennis wear. We'll plan on using this set for all tennis wear garments.

In your Magento backend:

1. Go to **Catalog | Attributes | Manage Attribute Sets**.
2. Click on **Add New Set** near the top of the screen.

3. Enter *Tennis Wear* for the **Name**.

4. To make creating an attribute set easier, Magento asks you to create your new set based on an existing set. For our example, choose *Shirts (General)* from the drop-down list (if you did not install the sample data, you have no other choice but *Default*).

5. Click on **Save Attribute Set**.

6. On the next screen are three columns. The first is the name of the attribute set. The second shows all the attributes assigned to this set, grouped into a folder hierarchy. The third column shows all unassigned attributes that can be added to the current set. For our attribute set, we want to add **garment_material**. Scroll down the second column until you see the folder titled **Description** and the attributes within it. Using your mouse, drag **garment_material** and position it anywhere within this folder, as shown in the next screenshot:

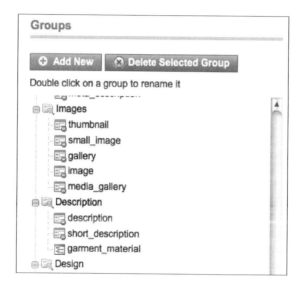

7. To remove an attribute from an attribute set, drag it to the list in the third column.

8. Click on **Save Attribute Set**.

9. You should see a warning at the top of your screen asking you to re-index Magento. Click on the link shown and re-index any required indexes.

We have now created a new attribute set to use for tennis wear which will include an attribute for the material. Furthermore, this attribute will be shown on the product details screen on the frontend and will be shown if a customer chooses to compare two or more garments.

Managing inventory

Most of the time, the manner in which you manage your product inventory will be dictated by the settings you make in **System | Configuration | Inventory**. However, as with most system configurations, you can override your choices for each product. Notice that inventory settings are Global in scope. Magento reasons that if you're managing inventory for a product in one store, you're also managing inventory in all stores for which the product might be assigned. Since some product inventory configurations are vague, let's go through each one. These are found in the Product Detail (**Catalog | Manage Products**) screen under the **Inventory** side tab:

- **Manage Stock**: Do you want Magento to keep track of products that are purchased and subtract them from the available inventory? If set to *No*, only **Minimum Qty Allowed in Shopping Cart** and **Maximum Qty Allowed in Shopping Cart** are available for configuration.

- **Qty**: A required field, this is the number of items you have on-hand to sell.

- **Qty for Item's Status to become Out of Stock**: If you want to keep some products in reserve, you can set a number below which, Magento will mark the product "Out of Stock." For example, if you want to keep five units in "reserve", Magento will show the item as "Out of Stock" by setting this field to 5 when the quantity remaining is 5 units.

- **Minimum Qty Allowed in Shopping Cart**: While *1* is a normal value, you might require a buyer to purchase a minimum number of a particular product.

- **Maximum Qty Allowed in Shopping Cart**: You may want to set a limit on the number of items that a buyer can purchase during a single transaction. There is no other limitation available, such as total purchased in one day or by one customer.

- **Qty Uses Decimals**: If you manage your product inventory in fractions of available inventory, set this to *Yes*.

- **Backorders**: If set to *Yes*, when a customer purchases a quantity of a product greater than available in inventory, they will be notified that some of the products will be on "backorder". If set to *No*, the customer cannot add more of a product to their shopping cart than is available in inventory.

- **Notify for Quantity Below**: As a store administrator, you may want to receive an e-mail alert whenever a product's inventory goes below a certain threshold; you might want to know when it's time to re-order stock.

- **Enable Qty Increments**: If you select *Yes*, the next field will appear, allowing you to set the increments at which a buyer can purchase your product.

- **Qty Increments**: In what quantity increments can the product be purchased?

> **Using "Quantity Increments" creatively**
>
> Let's assume you want to sell bottles of compressed air on your site, but in order to make enough margin to cover your overhead, you need a customer to buy a minimum of three bottles, although they can buy any quantity over that. In this case, you would enter 3 for **Minimum Qty Allowed in Shopping Cart**, *Yes* for **Enable Qty Increments**, and *1* for **Qty Increments**. For another example, you might want to sell these bottles at a minimum quantity of 6, with additional increments of 3 bottles at a time: set **Minimum Qty Allowed in Shopping Cart** to 6, **Enable Qty Increments** to *Yes*, and **Qty Increments** to 3.
>
> Unfortunately, you cannot configure Quantity Increments if you do not manage inventory. If you use a **drop shipper**, you may not be tracking inventory, as their inventory is available to other retailers as well. Still, you may want to require certain quantity increments. Hopefully, this will be added in future versions of Magento.

- **Stock Availability**: If you want the product saleable, select *In Stock*. When managing inventory, if the inventory level drops to zero (or below the floor you entered for **Qty for Item's Status to become Out of Stock**), the status for the product will automatically show as **Out of Stock** on the frontend, but will remain **In Stock** here. If you do not want the product to show as **In Stock** regardless of inventory level, choose *Out of Stock*.

Related products, up-sells, and cross-sells

For each product that you create in Magento, you have the opportunity to attract additional purchases from customers by linking products together. These cross-links allow you to encourage shoppers to consider buying products other than what they reviewed. In the brick-and-mortar world, we're constantly bombarded with similar promotions. For instance, if you go into the grocery store, you'll often find small, red coupon machines hanging off the shelves, encouraging you by their flashing red light to pull a coupon out while you're reaching the canned peaches that you came for. Throughout the store, placards and banners promote "2-for-1" specials, or "buy 1, get 1 free". The area around the checkout lane is crowded with magazines, razor blades, batteries, and gum, put there to catch your eye just as you're about to leave the store.

In a similar fashion, Magento allows you, the store administrator, to encourage shoppers to spend more during their online visit using related products, up-sells, and cross-sells. All three types are managed within the Product Detail screen.

Related products

As shown in the next screenshot, **related products** are other products that you want to show on a product details page as possible additional purchases, products *related* to the main product displayed. The customer can check any related products that they wish to add to the shopping cart at the same time that they add the main product. Therefore, related products are usually those for which a purchasing decision could be made without leaving the current product.

Some examples of related products might be:

- A carrying case for a smart phone
- An AC adapter for a portable speaker
- Leather cleaning kit for a sofa
- An extended warranty

A related product is one you want the customer to purchase *along with* the main product.

Up-sells

Like related products, **up-sells** are products that you wish to bring to your customer's attention. However, up-sells are generally considered to be products that may enhance the product purchased or help the customer notice other products to consider. Unlike related products, up-sells cannot be added to the shopping cart at the same time as the main product. Up-sells appear on the product details page, as shown in the next screenshot. They are generally considered products of a higher price or quality; products that you might want to encourage your customers to consider as an alternative to the currently viewed product.

Consider these up-sell product examples:

- A king-sized candy bar (as opposed to the normal size shown)
- A brass version of a nickel-plated door knob
- A 17" laptop, as opposed to the 15" model

Just as fast-food restaurants offer "up-sells" on meals, you can entice customers to make larger—or at least alternative—purchases by showcasing select products.

Cross-sells

Yet another way to promote additional products! Cross-sells appear on the shopping cart as other possible products to consider. The next screenshot shows a portion of the shopping cart with a cross-sell product shown for the added item:

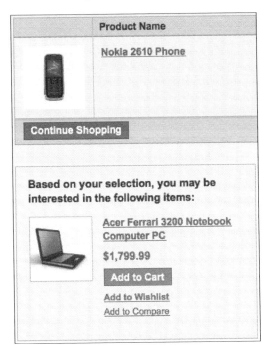

I consider cross-sells as products that we want to showcase to customers in order to introduce them to other product lines. For example, if we wanted to get camping enthusiasts to consider buying their backpacks from our store, we may offer select backpacks to those who buy camping stoves, sleeping bags, or hiking boots from us. Cross-sells are a creative way of encouraging shoppers to continue shopping after reaching the check-out page of your site.

Importing products

Creating products one-by-one is fine if you're only selling a few products, but many people choose Magento as a platform to sell hundreds and thousands of different products. Entering each product individually can take a long time, especially if you're writing unique product descriptions, uploading photos, and adding cross-linked products.

With Version 1.5, Magento has greatly improved the performance of product imports. In previous versions, importing thousands of products could take hours—literally. I once tried to import 19,000 products and the job took 20 hours to complete! The improvements to Magento importing have greatly decreased that time.

Really fast importing

Magento's importing tool is still not the fastest alternative available. While it works fine for a few thousand products, if you're building a store with tens of thousands of products, I highly recommend you take a look at **Magmi** [http://sourceforge.net/projects/magmi/]. Magmi is not so much an extension as it is a tool to help you rapidly import products—even complex types—in short order. In our use, Magmi imports products with photos at a rate of 2000 to 3000 per minute! Magmi is a freeware solution written by a French developer, and is constantly evolving. Go to the Magmi project [http://sourceforge.net/projects/magmi/] for the latest downloads and documentation.

The shortcut to importing products

After spending hundreds of hours wrestling with Magento's importing schemas over several versions of the platform, I'm happy to say that from Version 1.5 there is a shortcut to help you successfully import products.

Magento imports CSV files according to a specific layout scheme. Trying to configure an import file to accurately import a variety of different products, product types, attribute sets, and so on, will lead to many, many failed attempts as you try different ways of configuring the .csv to meet your needs. Therefore, my best advice is to do the following:

1. Enter at least one product into your store, representing the different types (simple, complex, bundle, and so on) that you will be using.
2. Fully enter the data for each product, including all options. You don't have to upload images however.
3. Go to **System | Import/Export | Export** in your backend.
4. Export a product .csv file to your computer (in previous Magento versions, this export would be placed on your server and you would have had to FTP in order for your server to retrieve it).
5. Open the downloaded .csv file in Excel or Numbers.

Now, you can easily see how each type of product is configured in the export file. Using this format, you can easily add additional products, simply by following a similar pattern.

Notice that for products with various options, particularly configurable products, only the differences between each iteration are included on the rows below the main product row. Never repeat any other fields that are the same between variations. A unique SKU is required of each product though.

To import images, you must upload the images to your server in the /media/import folder. If the /import folder doesn't exist, create it. Put the name of the image file in the image columns of your import .csv file (don't include any path). Magento will pick the image out of the /media/import folder, resize it as needed, and store it within the /images/catalog folder hierarchy. Never use capitals, spaces, or other strange characters in your image names; only the letters a through z, the numbers 0 through 9, and the underscore.

The most important thing to remember is to remove any unused columns before importing. For example, if you are not going to include categories in your import, leave that column out. This is especially important if you are re-importing or importing product updates. If you leave a column blank, then Magento will enter a blank value for that column in your product record. Oops!

Summary

Selling online begins with your products. Your products have to be presented well, and in logical categories. Furthermore, Magento gives you additional powerful tools for promoting your products to potential customers.

In this chapter, we:

- Learned about how catalogs and categories relate to each other, and to your stores.
- Learned about the different types of products that can be sold in a Magento store.
- Went in-depth into how to create and manage attributes and attribute sets.
- Discussed inventory management configurations.
- Learned a shortcut for configuring product imports.

Getting a handle on how the complexity of categories and products in Magento is actually one of its greatest strengths, puts you in a better position to leverage the remaining topics in this book toward encouraging more sales from your visiting customers. Next, we turn our attention to *grabbing* attention: how to theme your Magento store.

4
Designs and Themes

Selling online, as with brick and mortar retailing, is more than simply having products to offer to customers. Buyers make purchases based on many things apart from the item itself. Customers want to understand the purpose of the retailer and have confidence that the seller is legitimate, safe, and honest. Corporations have spent billions over the years creating this understanding among their active and potential customers through logos, design, copy, and service. Creating this understanding is called **branding**.

For an online store, branding is very important. However, unlike the offline shopper who drives to a store, parks, and enters the store to spend several minutes shopping, an online shopper may click to your online store, spend a few seconds to determine if they wish to remain, and leave to visit another website. Therefore, your store's brand—its graphics, copy, and function—must address the following in a matter of seconds:

- Does this online store have what I'm looking for? Can I easily find what they sell?
- Do I trust this seller if I've never heard of them before?
- Does the retailer make it easy for me to shop and purchase?
- Does it appear that the store owner is interested in helping me buy?

Magento gives you, or your client, the functional tools and systems to provide a powerfully rich shopping experience to your customers. It cannot, however, provide the branding aspects relating to design. You have to craft the outward appearance in such a way that it will communicate to the potential buyer the feelings of convenience, product selection, and security.

In this chapter, we will teach you:

- The Magento theme structure
- How to install third-party themes
- How to customize themes to create your own unique look and feel

The Magento theme structure

In *Chapter 3, Managing Products*, we discussed the GWS methodology. As we have learned, Magento allows you to customize many store aspects at some or all of the GWS levels.

The same holds true for themes. You can specify the look and feel of your stores at the **Global**, **Website**, or **Store** levels (themes can be applied for individual store views relating to a store) by assigning a specific theme.

In Magento, a group of related themes is referred to as a **design package**. Design packages contain files that control various functional elements that are common among the themes within the package. By default, Magento Community installs two design packages:

- **Base package**: A special package that contains all the default elements for a Magento installation (we will discuss this in more detail in a moment)
- **Default package**: This contains the layout elements of the default store (look and feel), which we have seen already in previous chapters

Themes within a design package contain the various elements that determine the look and feel of the site: layout files, templates, CSS, images, and JavaScript. Each design package must have at least one default theme, but can contain other theme variants. You can include any number of theme variants within a design package and use them, for example, for seasonal purposes (that is, holidays, back-to-school, and so on).

The following image shows the relationship between design packages and themes:

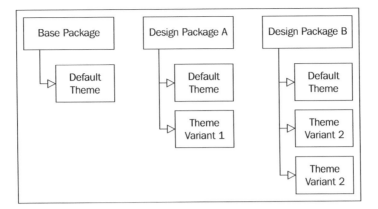

A design package and theme can be specified at the **Global**, **Website,** or **Store** levels.

 Most Magento users will use the same design package for a website and all descendant stores. Usually, related stores within a website business share very similar functional elements, as well as similar style features. This is not mandatory; you are free to specify a completely different design package and theme for each store view within your website hierarchy.

The theme structure

Magento divides themes into two group of files: **templating** and **skin**. Templating files contain the HTML, PHTML, and PHP code that determines the functional aspects of the pages in your Magento website. Skin files are made of CSS, image, and JavaScript files that give your site its outward design.

Ingeniously, Magento further separates these areas by putting them into different directories of your installation:

- Templating files are stored in the `app/design` directory, where the extra security of this section protects the functional parts of your site design

- Skin files are stored within the `skin` directory (at the root level of the installation), and can be granted a higher permission level, as these are the files that are delivered to a visitor's browser for rendering the page

Templating hierarchy

Frontend theme template files (the files used to produce your store's pages) are stored within three subdirectories:

- `layout`: These are the XML files that contain the various core information that defines various areas of a page. These files also contain meta and encoding information.

- `template`: This stores the PHTML files (HTML files that contain PHP code and processed by the PHP server engine) used for constructing the visual structure of the page.

- `locale`: In *Chapter 3, Managing Products,* we talked about adding files within this directory to provide additional language translations for site elements, such as labels and messages.

Magento has a distinct path for storing templating files used for your website: `app/design/frontend/[Design Package]/[Theme]/`.

Skin hierarchy

The skin files for a given design package and theme are subdivided into the following:

- `css`: This stores the CSS stylesheets, and, in some cases, related image files that are called by CSS files (this is not an acceptable convention, but I have seen some designers do this)

- `images`: This contains the JPG, PNG, and GIF files used in the display of your site

- `js`: This contains the JavaScript files that are specific to a theme (JavaScript files used for core functionality are kept in the `js` directory at the root level)

The path for the frontend skin files is: `skin/frontend/[Design Package]/[Theme]/`.

The concept of theme fallback

A very important and brilliant aspect of Magento is what is called the **Magento theme fallback model**. Basically, this concept means that when building a page, Magento first looks to the assigned theme for a store. If the theme is missing any necessary templating or skin files, Magento then looks to the required default theme within the assigned design package. If the file is not found there, Magento finally looks into the default theme of the Base design package. For this reason, the Base design package is never to be altered or removed; it is the failsafe for your site. The following flowchart outlines the process by which Magento finds the necessary files for fulfilling a page rendering request.

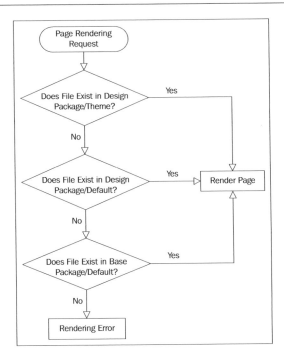

This model also gives the designers some tremendous assistance. When a new theme is created, it only has to contain those elements that are different from what is provided by the Base package. For example, if all parts of a desired site design are similar to the Base theme, except for the graphic appearance of the site, a new theme can be created simply by adding new CSS and image files to the new theme (stored within the skin directory). Any new CSS files will need to be included in the local. xml file for your theme (we will discuss the local.xml file later in this chapter). If the design requires different layout structures, only the changed layout and template files need to be created; everything that remains the same need not be duplicated.

While previous versions of Magento were built with fallback mechanisms, only in the current versions has this become a true and complete fallback. In the earlier versions, the fallback was to the default theme within a package, not to the Base design package. Therefore, each default theme within a package had to contain all the files of the Base package. If Magento Base files were updated in subsequent software versions, these changes had to be redistributed manually to each additional design package within a Magento installation. With Magento CE 1.4 and above, upgrades to the Base package automatically enhance all design packages.

If you are careful not to alter the Base design package, then future upgrades to the core functionality of Magento will not break your installation. You will have access to the new improvements based on your custom design package or theme, making your installation virtually upgrade proof. For the same reason, never install a custom theme inside the Base design package.

Default installation design packages and themes

In a new, clean Magento Community installation, you are provided with the following design packages and themes:

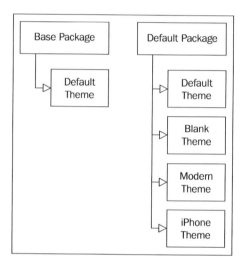

Depending on your needs, you could add additional custom design packages, or custom themes within the default design package:

- If you're going to install a group of related themes, you should probably create a new design package, containing a default theme as your fallback theme

- On the other hand, if you're using only one or two themes based on the features of the default design package, you can install the themes within the default design package hierarchy

I like to make sure that whatever I customize can be undone, if necessary. It's difficult for me to make changes to the core, installed files; I prefer to work on duplicate copies, preserving the originals in case I need to revert back. After re-installing Magento for the umpteenth time because I had altered too many core files, I learned the hard way!

As Magento Community installs a basic variety of good theme variants from which to start, the first thing you should do before adding or altering theme components is to duplicate the default design package files, renaming the duplicate to an appropriate name, such as a description of your installation (for example, Acme or Sports). Any changes you make within this new design package will not alter the originally installed components, thereby allowing you to revert any or all of your themes to the originals.

Your new theme hierarchy might now look as follows:

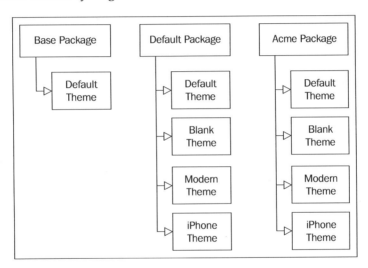

When creating new packages, you also need to create new folders in the /skin directory to match your directory hierarchy in the /app/design directory.

Likewise, if you decide to use one of the installed default themes as the basis for designing a new custom theme, duplicate and rename the theme to preserve the original as your fallback.

The new Blank theme

A fairly recent default installed theme is **Blank**. If your customization to your Magento stores is primarily one of colors and graphics, this is not a bad theme to use as a starting point. As the name implies, it has a pretty stark layout, as shown in the following screenshot. However, it does give you all the basic structures and components.

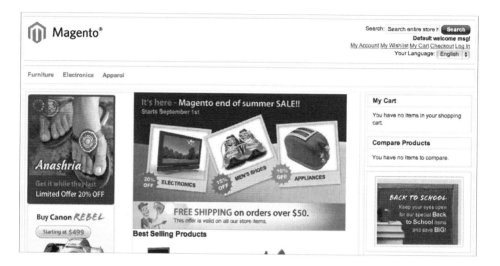

Using images and CSS styles, you can go a long way to creating a good-looking, functional website, as shown in the next screenshot for www.aviationlogs.com:

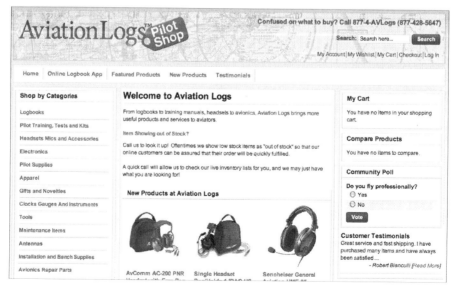

When duplicating any design package or theme, don't forget that each of them is defined by directories under /app/design/frontend/ and /skin/frontend/.

Installing third-party themes

In most cases, Magento users who are beginners will explore hundreds of the available Magento themes created by third-party designers. There are many free ones available, but most are sold by dedicated designers.

Shopping for themes

One of the great good/bad aspects of Magento is the third-party themes. The architecture of the Magento theme model gives knowledgeable theme designers tremendous abilities to construct themes that are virtually upgrade proof, while possessing powerful enhancements. Unfortunately, not all designers have either upgraded older themes properly or created new themes fully honoring the fallback model. If the older fallback model is still used for current Magento versions, upgrades to the Base package could adversely affect your theme.

Therefore, as you review third-party themes, take time to investigate how the designer constructs their themes. Most provide some type of site demo. As you learn more about using themes, you'll find it easier to analyze third-party themes.

Apart from a few free themes offered through the Magento website, most of them require that you install the necessary files manually, by FTP or SFTP to your server. Every third-party theme I have ever used has included some instructions on how to install the files to your server. However, allow me to offer the following helpful guidelines:

- When using FTP/SFTP to upload theme files, use the merge function so that only additional files are added to each directory, instead of replacing entire directories. If you're not sure whether your FTP client provides merge capabilities, or not sure how to configure for merge, you will need to open each directory in the theme and upload the individual files to the corresponding directories on your server.

- If you have set your CSS and JavaScript files to **merge**, under **System | Configuration | Developer**, you should turn merging off while installing and modifying your theme.

- After uploading themes or any component files (for example, templates, CSS, or images), clear the Magento caches under **System | Cache Management** in your backend.

- Disable your Magento cache while you install and configure themes. While not critical, it will allow you to see changes immediately instead of having to constantly clear the Magento cache. You can disable the cache under **System | Cache Management** in the backend.

- If you wish to make any changes to a theme's individual file, make a duplicate of the original file before making your changes. That way, if something goes awry, you can always re-install the duplicated original.

- If you have followed the earlier advice to duplicate the Default design package before customizing, instructions to install files within /app/ design/frontend/default/ and /skin/frontend/default/ should be interpreted as /app/design/frontend/*[your design package name]*/ and / skin/frontend/*[your design package name]*/, respectively. As most of the new Magento users don't duplicate the Default design package, it's common for theme designers to instruct users to install new themes and files within the Default design package. (We know better, now, don't we?)

Creating variants

Let's assume that we have created a new design package called *outdoor_package*. Within this design package, we duplicate the Blank theme and call it *outdoor_ theme*. Our new design package file hierarchy, in both /app/design/ and /skin/ frontend/ might resemble the following hierarchy:

```
app/
   design/
      frontend/
         default/
            blank/
            modern/
            iphone/
         outdoor_package/
            outdoor_theme/

skin/
   frontend/
      default/
         blank/
            blue/
         french/
```

```
      german/
      modern/
      iphone/
   outdoor_package/
      outdoor_theme/
```

However, let's also take one more customization step here. Since Magento separates the template structure from the skin structure—the layout from the design, so to speak—we could create variations of a theme that are simply controlled by CSS and images, by creating more than one skin. For Acme, we might want to have our English language store in a blue color scheme, but our French language store in a green color scheme. We could take the acme/skin directory and duplicate it, renaming both for the new colors:

```
app/
   design/
      frontend/
         default/
            blank/
            modern/
            iphone/
         outdoor_package/
            outdoor_theme/

   skin/
      frontend/
         default/
            blank/
               blue/
            french/
            german/
            modern/
            iphone/
         outdoor_package/
            outdoor_blue/
            outdoor_green/
```

Before we continue, let's go over something which is especially relevant to what we just created.

For our outdoor theme, we created two skin variants: blue and green. However, what if the difference between the two is only one or two files? If we make changes to other files that would affect both color schemes, but which are otherwise the same for both, this would create more work to keep both color variations in sync, right?

Remember, with the Magento fallback method, if your site calls on a file, it first looks into the assigned theme, then the default theme within the same design package, and, finally, within the Base design package. Therefore, in this example, you could use the default skin, under `/skin/frontend/outdoor_package/default/` to contain all files common to both blue and green. Only include those files that will forever remain different to each of them within their respective skin directories.

Assigning themes

As mentioned earlier, you can assign design packages and themes at any level of the GWS hierarchy. As with any configuration, the choice depends on the level you wish to assign control. **Global** configurations affect the entire Magento installation. **Website** level choices set the default for all subordinant store views, which can also have their own theme specifics, if desired.

Let's walk through the process of assigning a custom design package and themes. For the sake of this exercise, let's continue with our Outdoor theme, as described earlier. If you recall from *Chapter 2, Successful Magento Installation*, we created an **Outdoor** website and store, with two store views for English and French:

We're going to now assign our Outdoor theme to the **Outdoor** website and store views. Our first task is to assign the design package and theme to the website as the default for all subordinant store views:

1. Go to **System | Configuration | General | Design** in your Magento backend.

2. In the **Current Configuration Scope** drop-down menu, choose **Outdoor Products**.

3. As shown in the following screenshot, enter the name of your design package, template, layout, and skin. You will have to uncheck the boxes labeled **Use Default** beside each field you wish to use.

4. Click on the **Save Config** button.

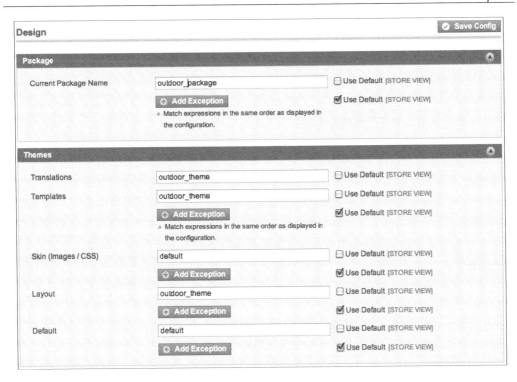

The reason you enter **default** in the fields, as shown in the previous screenshot, is to provide the fallback protection I described earlier. Magento needs to know where to look for any files that may be missing from your theme files.

Creative translations

In *Chapter 2, Successful Magento Installation*, we learned how to create store views in different languages. But, as you can see in the previous screenshot, you have the ability to assign a theme in a field called **Translations**. This is a very under-documented, yet creative feature of Magento, so let's tackle the discussion now.

First, the purpose of **Translations** is to allow you to specify a different output for various text elements of your site. With the language translation files we installed in *Chapter 2, Successful Magento Installation*, a number of standard text labels, such as **My Account**, **Checkout**, and so on are translated into the desired language. These language files reside in your /app/locale directory and are triggered by selecting the language in the **System** | **Configuration** | **General** | **Locale Options** panel in your Magento backend. The **Translations** field we are specifying in the **Design** | **Themes** panel looks for a file called translation.csv, residing in your theme's locale directory.

If you have installed language files, as we discussed in *Chapter 3, Managing Products*, you'll also find a great number of `translation.csv` files under `/app/locale`. These are the core language files for both the frontend and backend of your installation, and are fully editable if you wish to change a particular phrase.

The default installation's `translation.csv` file contains one translation line:

```
"Keep your eyes open for our special Back to School items and save A
LOT!","Keep your eyes open for our special Back to School items and
save A LOT!"
```

Huh? Both phrases in this line, separated by a comma, are the same. But, ignore this line for now. The purpose of this file is to set out the format for which you can specify various text translations. The key here is to realize that translations do not have to be from one language to another, although that is a primary purpose when these `translation.csv` files are located within a language folder (for example, `fr_FR`).

So how can this file benefit you as the site administrator or designer? Imagine you wanted every place on the site that said "New Customers" to now say "New Shoppers". It would be a tedious process to go through every Magento file that contains the phrase "New Customers" and change it to "New Shoppers". Believe me, it's not a task you want to do more than once.

On the other hand, if you wanted to change **NEW CUSTOMERS** (as shown in the following screenshot) to **NEW SHOPPERS**, you simply add `"New Customers","New Shoppers"` to your `translations.csv` file:

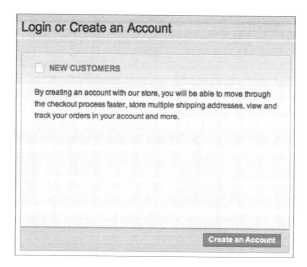

Magento will automatically do the conversions for you on the fly, as shown in the following screenshot:

With the use of theme variants, explained in the following section, you could specify translations pertinent to holidays, such as "New Customers" to "New Holiday Shoppers", or "Welcome" to "Happy Holidays".

Using theme variants

Besides the obvious use of different themes within a package for different looks among store views, theme variants can be used to provide alternative frontend layouts based on date, such as holiday shopping season, or device, such as smartphone or tablet.

Scheduling a theme variant

It would be painful if changes that affect your public site content had to be manually turned on at the exact date and time you wished. For products, you can schedule price changes to automatically take effect between any two dates and times (you could have a one-hour sale price!) simply by adding the date/time configuration in the product detail screen.

Likewise, you can schedule changes in your stores' themes to take effect while you sleep! Using the following steps, you can schedule a theme variant based on a date:

1. Go to **System | Design** in your Magento backend.
2. Click on **Add Design Change**.
3. Select the store view you wish to change.
4. Choose from the **Custom Design** drop-down, the theme variant you want.
5. Enter the **Date From** and **Date To** date and times, for the period of time you want the change to take effect.
6. Click on **Save**.

Customizing themes

I've never met a person yet that installed a theme and was ready to launch their Magento store without wanting or even needing changes to be made to the store design. It's natural, as a store needs to have its own personality, its own brand. In this section, we hope to uncover many of the mysteries of how Magento controls a store's look and feel through layered components that, once you understand how they work together, will give you a tremendous ability to make your Magento store a unique, productive online retail destination.

Customizing skins

The easiest way of changing the look and feel of your Magento store is by modifying existing stylesheets and graphic images. As we have learned, these are stored within your theme's directory in the `/skin/frontend/` part of your Magento installation.

 As always, I highly recommend that you make duplicates of the original theme files before making changes. Just to be safe!

Since Magento defines webpage areas using `<div>` tags, you can find it fairly easy to modify the style of the site by identifying the `<div>` tags—as well as other HTML tags such as `<p>`, `<form>`, and `<input>`—and editing the CSS styles that are assigned to them.

Finding CSS

 While you can view the source code of a webpage in any browser, there are better ways of identifying not only the HTML elements of a page, but the exact CSS style(s) that are controlling how that component appears.

For Firefox browsers, you can install the Firebug plugin (`http://getfirebug.com`). For Safari and Chrome users, this functionality is included with the browser. Another great tool for Firefox users is the **Webdeveloper** add-on (`https://addons.mozilla.org/pt-br/firefox/addon/web-developer/`). These tools allow you to select an element on the page and view in another window what the styling rules are that apply to the element. Once you know that, you can easily find the CSS style statement in the theme's CSS stylesheets and make any changes you wish.

Customizing layouts

Page layouts in Magento are managed by XML files that control how the various components on a page are to be assembled. Think of layout files as the blueprints of your site, in that they contain the instructions that direct how various content blocks and template files are combined to produce the structural blocks that define the final output.

Let's take a visual look at how structural blocks and content blocks are combined on a typical page, by analyzing a category page captured from our sample data default installation:

Now, let's look at this page, with the structural blocks (left) and content blocks (right) shown as overlays on this category page:

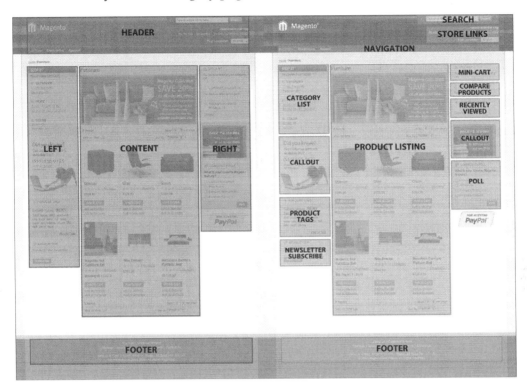

Structural and content blocks

The preceding screenshot on the left shows the outlines of the structural blocks. For a Magento page, they are the containers that dictate the positions of content blocks, as shown in the previous screenshot on the right. There are five primary structural blocks: header, left column, right column, content, and footer. Technically, a page can have any number of structural blocks, but these are the basic blocks used by most Magento themes.

Structural blocks are defined in the `page.xml` file located within the `layout/` directory of a theme (for example, `app/design/frontend/base/default/layout/page.xml`). Default page templates, called by this file, are stored within the `/template/page/` directory.

Content blocks represent the actual layout content that will appear on a web page. Where functionality contents (such as category listings, product listings, or shopping cart) appear, content blocks interpret the output into the text, graphics, and styles visible on the web page. The template files that contain the markup code for the content blocks are also stored within the /template/ directory (some HTML code, however, does come from the actual code output from the /app/code directory files).

Expertly controlling layouts

Magento newcomers, particularly designers, often feel a bit lost among the many layout and template files that comprise a Magento theme. However, with a bit of study (this book!) and adherence to a few best practices, anyone can become a Magento design aficionado.

First, keep in mind the concept of the Magento fallback method we previously covered. Layouts are dictated by the most forward layer. This means that if the chosen theme lacks a needed layout or template file, Magento will look into the default directory for the design package, then into the base/default directory, where, unless you've been naughty and changed anything, Magento will at last find any missing components.

As a designer, this means that you can change layout structures and blocks by creating or editing files within your theme directory, and focus on overriding any base theme behaviors. In short, a theme has to have only those components that are different from the base design package.

I want to emphasize the enormity of this concept. When I wear my designer's hat, I don't have to replicate all of the many layout and template files when creating a theme. I only have to include those most likely few files that will define the delta or difference between the base package and my new theme.

This, more robust fallback method (when compared to previous Magento versions), has not been completely absorbed by third-party theme producers. You may find some themes that have many files that really define no difference from the base package. This practice does not conform to Magento's best practices, as the core Magento updates cannot be reflected properly in the theme files. In general, we look for themes structures—whether third-party or home-grown—to add only those files necessary to provide the differences between the default layouts and the customized design.

When looking for a file to edit for your intended change, first look into your theme directory. If the file is not there, look into the default directory within your theme's design package. If you find the file there, copy it into the same relative position within your theme directory.

Layout files control the various Magento modules, such as `Sales`, `Customers`, and `Catalog`, by using a layout XML file defining their structural blocks, content blocks, and functional components. You can find all of the default layout files under `/app/design/frontend/base/default/layout`. At the time when I wrote this chapter, there were 36 layout files in addition to `page.xml`. Add-on extensions may add additional layout files to this list.

Now, here's where it may get just a bit complex: each layout file contains **handles**: groups of block definitions that generally correspond with a type of page produced by Magento. Handles can either be labeled `<default>`, meaning they will generally apply to all rendered pages, or they will have specific labels, such as `<catalog_product_compare_index>`, which means they apply only to those pages on which that particular handle is called by the template file.

To get a better understanding of handles, let's dissect an example handle found in the `catalog.xml` file:

```
<default>
<reference name="left">
<block type="core/template" name="left.permanent.callout"
template="callouts/left_col.phtml">
<action method="setImgSrc"><src>images/media/col_left_callout.jpg</src></action>
<action method="setImgAlt" translate="alt" module="catalog"><alt>Our
customer service is available 24/7. Call us at (555) 555-0123.</alt></action>
<action method="setLinkUrl"><url>checkout/cart</url></action>
</block>
</reference>
```

From this code snippet, we can find out quite a bit about what it does to affect your layout:

- `<default>` is the name of the handle. This name, which should never be changed (Magento relies on this name to process the functionality tied to it), suggests that it is used on all pages relating to the display of products.

- <reference> tells us into what structural or content block the enclosed content is to be defined. For example, <reference name="footer_links"> suggests that the output generated by the enclosed code will be placed within a block defined elsewhere as footer_links. We can use these references to modify where various elements may appear on a page, as we will explore a little later in this chapter.

As you look within each <reference> tag, you will find a collection of <block> and <action> tags. Let's look a bit more closely at this snippet:

```
<reference name="left">
<block type="core/template" name="left.permanent.callout"
template="callouts/left_col.phtml">
<action method="setImgSrc"><src>images/media/col_left_callout.jpg</
src></action>
<action method="setImgAlt" translate="alt" module="catalog"><alt>Our
customer service is available 24/7. Call us at (555) 555-0123.</alt></
action>
<action method="setLinkUrl"><url>checkout/cart</url></action>
</block>
</reference>
```

This particular section of code defines a block called left.permanent.callout. By enclosing the block with the <reference> tag, this file is telling Magento that this content block needs to be rendered within another block called left, which, as we learned earlier, is one of the default structural blocks. More specifically, left is the name of the left column structural block.

> While it may appear to be a bit inside out, it is the <block> tag that we are most interested in. The <block> defines the content. The <reference> tag merely designates where the content block is to be placed. We can change the <reference> tag without affecting the output of the content block.

The <block> tag also specifies a template file, callouts/left_col.phtml, that contains the HTML and PHP code defining the visual output for this block (not all blocks have related .phtml files, though).

This is the main portion of the code contained within the `left_col.phtml` template file:

```
<div class="block block-banner">
<div class="block-content">
<?php if(strtolower(substr($this->getLinkUrl(),0,4))==='http'): ?>
<a href="<?php echo $this->getLinkUrl() ?>" title="<?php echo $this-
>__($this->getImgAlt()) ?>">
<?php elseif($this->getLinkUrl()): ?>
<a href="<?php echo $this->getUrl($this->getLinkUrl()) ?>"
title="<?php echo $this->__($this->getImgAlt()) ?>">
<?php endif; ?>
<img src="<?php echo $this->getSkinUrl($this->getImgSrc()) ?>"<?php
if(!$this->getLinkUrl()): ?> title="<?php echo $this->__($this-
>getImgAlt()) ?>"<?php endif; ?> alt="<?php echo $this->__($this-
>getImgAlt()) ?>" />
<?php if($this->getLinkUrl()): ?>
</a>
<?php endif ?>
</div>
</div>
```

The `<action>` tags in the `<block>` tag tell Magento to perform certain actions as directed by the method attribute. In this case, we have three actions to perform:

- `<action method="setImgSrc">` sets a file path called `ImgSrc`
- `<action method="setImgAlt" translate="alt" module="catalog">` creates a text value called `ImgAlt`
- `<action method="setLinkUrl">` creates a file path called `LinkUrl`

With these values created by the block, the assigned template file, `left_col.phtml`, can use these values to create the output (refer to the previous code snippet):

- `$this->getImgSrc()` uses the value called `ImgSrc`, which in our example is `images/media/col_left_callout.jpg`
- `$this->getImgAlt()` uses the `ImgAlt` value, or `Our customer service is available 24/7. Call us at (555) 555-0123`
- `$this->getLinkUrl()` uses `LinkUrl`, or `checkout/cart` as the link path to the target file

By changing the values set within the `catalog.xml` file, you do not have to change the template file unless you want to change the HTML layout elements to suit your needs.

Rather than changing the `catalog.xml` file, it's much, much better to override the original block by inserting the revised block into the `local.xml` file. Hang on, as we will discuss the `local.xml` file in the next section.

Perfect use of translations

Over the years, I've seen so many people struggle with the fact that the default Magento themes contain permanent callouts such as the one we examined previously. It's easy enough to substitute the graphic by simply replacing the default graphic, `col_left_callout.jpg` (located at `/skin/frontend/default/default/images/media`). However, Magento users who are not familiar with XML and PHP, much less the Magento architecture, find the ALT tag content difficult to change. Obviously, your store's phone number is not (555) 555-0123.

Using the `translate.csv` file in your theme, which we discussed earlier, you could simply add a line such as: Our customer service is available 24/7. Call us at (555) 555-0123., If you have any questions, or need assistance, call us at (888) 555-9999, or whatever your actual phone number is. Keep in mind that translations only apply if the entire text element matches the translation file: you can't simply translate the phone number without specifying the entire text portion.

The attributes for the `<block>` tag include:

- `type`: This defines the functional purpose of the block. Do not modify this.

- `name`: This is used by other blocks as a reference to which the block is to be assigned.

- `before` and `after`: This attribute can be used to position the block before or after other referenced blocks that will be placed within the same referenced block. `before="-"` and `after="-"` position the block at the very top or very bottom of the referenced block.

- `template`: This calls the template file that supplies the output functionality of the block.

- `action`: A subordinant tag that controls functionality, such as setting values, loading or unloading JavaScript, and more.

- `as`: The name which is used by templates to call the block. For example, `getChildHtml('left.permanent.callout')` would include the block within the template file.

It's important to remember that like all XML tags, `<block>` tags must be closed. That is, the tag much either be matched with `</block>` or, where there are no child tags, closed with `/>`, such as in `<block name="call-out" />`.

Using the reference tag to relocate blocks

In our previous example, the graphic callout defined by the `left.permanent.callout` block was designed to be placed within the left structural block, not by the name of the block, but rather by the `<reference name="left">` tag. The block could be named just about anything; it's the `reference` tag that dictates into which structural block on the page the block will be rendered.

If we wanted this block to be positioned within the right structural block, we simply change the `reference` tag to `<reference name="right">`. By using `reference` tags, we can position our content blocks into the general areas of the page. To refine the placement, we can use the block attributes of `before` and `after`, or call the block from within a template file using the `as` attribute.

Customizing the local layout file

At this point, we've discussed how, by copying and modifying a few files for your theme, you can change the appearance of various blocks within your layout. With the release of Magento 1.4 and above, you have one additional tool at your disposal: the local layout file. In fact, this often-overlooked new feature is perhaps one of the most powerful layout tools in your arsenal!

By creating a file called `local.xml` and placing it within the `/layout` directory of your theme, you can alter your layout by turning off any blocks defined by the base package `page.xml` file. In other words, if you don't need or want the `left.permanent.callout` block, you can simply tell Magento to ignore it or, in Magento-ese, remove it. You can also use the local layout file to reposition blocks (as we described previously) or re-define specific handles. In short, it's a great way to make changes to your layouts without having to get deep into the various layout files we discussed earlier.

The first step is to create a `local.xml` file, if one doesn't already exist, and place it within the `/app/design/frontend/[design package]/[design theme]/layout` directory. Add the following code to this text file:

```xml
<?xml version="1.0" ?>
<layout
  <default>
    <!-- Put block overrides here -->
  </default>
</layout>
```

Within this small collection of code, you can add blocks and handles, as well as specialized statements. For example, to remove the `callout` block with which we have been working, add the following code between the `<default>` and `</default>` tags of your `local.xml` file:

```xml
<remove name="left.permanent.callout" />
```

And just like that, the `callout` block is no longer appearing on your site.

On the other hand, if we want to move our `callout` to another layout position—say, to the right column—and not remove it (the previous code would remove the block entirely from use), but rather unset it from the original position and place it in the new position, then use the following code:

```xml
<reference name="left">
<action method="unsetChild">
<name>left.permanent.callout</name>
</action>
</reference>
<reference name="right">
<block type="core/template" name="left.permanent.callout"
template="callouts/left_col.phtml">
<action method="setImgSrc"><src>images/media/col_left_callout.jpg</src></action>
<action method="setImgAlt" translate="alt" module="catalog"><alt>Our
customer service is available 24/7. Call us at (555) 555-0123.</alt></action>
<action method="setLinkUrl"><url>checkout/cart</url></action>
</block>
</reference>
```

The scope of possibilities for using the local layout file is quite extensive. As you begin exploring the use of this file, I would offer the following advice:

- Use the `<remove>` tag to completely disable blocks rather than removing them from layout files. If you don't have any other use for the layout file that contains the block, then you won't even have the need to copy it from the base package into your theme.

- Use `<action method="unsetChild">` to simply disable the block from the current layout, but allow it to be used in another position.

- If you want to modify a block or handle, copy it from the base package layout file and paste it into your `local.xml` file. Then make the changes you want to make. Again, this negates the need for replicating the layout files, and it gives you a much quicker ability to make modifications and test them to see if they are behaving as you expected.

Summary

Creating the look and feel of a new Magento store is, for those designers among us, one of the most exciting aspects of creating a new website. However, as we have seen, to give store owners the level of power and functionality that Magento affords, designers can no longer build static HTML pages, slap in a bit of PHP, and upload it to the server. With high levels of functionality come higher levels of architectural complexity.

Fortunately, the complexity of Magento is not nearly as daunting once you understand the methodologies of how pages are built, rendered, and styled. I struggled initially to fully understand this system. However, today I feel very comfortable navigating the design-related components of Magento after taking the time to understand how it all pieces together. Today, you have the added advantage of a much improved architecture, as well as this book in your hands.

Hopefully, I've also shown you that in most cases, if you want an extensively customized theme, you really don't have to start from scratch. By using the existing default themes, or using a third-party theme, you can do some quite extensive customizations simply by modifying a few key files.

Experiment and have fun!

In this chapter, we:

- Explored the Magento theme architecture, learning how the Magento fallback method works to ensure our pages always have something to show
- Covered the installation and configuration of themes into our Magento store structure
- Learned how to modify our themes by understanding the use of layouts, handles, and blocks
- Were introduced to a fairly new and very powerful tool: the local layout file

You will no doubt want to spend some time exploring the concepts of this chapter. I don't blame you. Just writing this chapter makes me want to dig into a new design!

When you are ready to move on, we will begin the process of configuring your store for what it is intended: to sell.

5
Configuring to Sell

If you've been following the instructions in this book, chapter by chapter, then by now you will have created a working, accessible online store front. *Ready to take orders now?*

Not just yet. There's still more to do before you can swing open the virtual doors to your new Magento store. Specifically, we need to:

- Understand the Magento sales process
- Configure payment gateways to allow you to take online credit card payments
- Set up how your products will be shipped
- Configure sales tax rules
- Create customized outgoing e-mails

If you're the developer or designer of a Magento-powered site, this is usually the time when you consult with your client—the store owner—to learn how they want to take payments, charge for shipping, and offer promotional discounts. Once you understand the concepts in this chapter, you'll be well prepared to ask the right questions.

For store owners and administrators, this chapter will give you insights into what can be managed with Magento. Fortunately, there are few limitations to Magento. I am, however, consistently amazed at the various ways retailers price and vend their products. Hopefully, whatever unique selling programs you currently employ can be replicated online with your Magento store. I'm betting they can.

The sales process

If you've shopped online before, you no doubt have some understanding of the usual online sales process:

1. You browse and find a product that you want to purchase.

2. You "add" the product to your virtual shopping cart.

3. When you're finished shopping, you go to a *checkout* page.

4. In most online stores, you will first enter your billing and shipping addresses.

5. From this information, various shipping alternatives are presented, from which you choose the most appropriate for your needs and budget.

6. Next, you choose a payment method and enter your credit card information.

7. After reviewing your order details, you commit to the purchase, and moments later you receive confirmation that your order has been processed. You usually receive an e-mail receipt of your purchase.

8. After a day or so, you receive another e-mail announcing that your order has been shipped. This e-mail may also include package tracking numbers so that you can follow the progress of your package from "distribution to doorstep".

The Magento sales process

Magento duplicates this **sales process** in much the same way. For our purposes, though, we need to understand what happens after the customer commits to the order, for that is when the store administrator's participation is required.

The next chart illustrates both the **frontend** and **backend** steps of the Magento **sales process**:

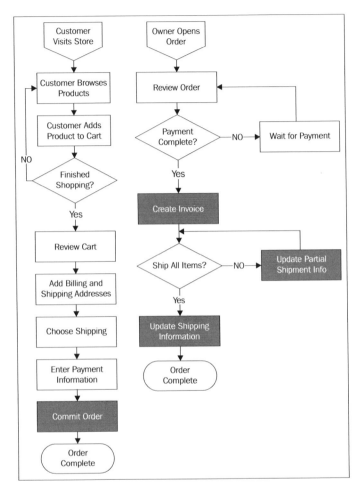

The black squares with white type are steps that generally create an e-mail to the customer.

As we'll see in this chapter, there are occasional variations to this process, but in general, the Magento sales process is pretty straightforward. What you'll find impressive is the scope of Magento's ability to give you a wider latitude on adjusting the sales process to meet your particular needs. For instance, if you're selling downloadable products, such as e-books, music, or software, you don't need the shipping process steps. Yet, if you sell proprietary digital media, you will need to manage the distribution of the products to your customers. For instance, to prevent unlimited downloads.

Managing backend orders

Before mapping out the business rules that you will use to configure Magento, it's helpful to see and understand how **orders** are processed in the Magento backend. Many times, developers and administrators new to Magento rush to configure the myriad of settings (which we will be covering in this chapter) without fully realizing how those choices might impact the overall sales process. It's understandable because most will want to test the ordering system with all the settings in place. It's a bit of a catch-22: you have no orders to use to understand the configurations, yet without the configurations, you can't test the ordering process.

Fortunately, a basic Magento install with the sample data (again with the sample data? Yes!) gives you the basic configurations to allow you to place some sample orders and review the order process.

Give it a whirl!

If you've installed the sample data, or you already have a store configured to accept some type of test payments, you should spend some time placing and processing orders. Try any number of different combinations. Ask your colleagues to place dummy orders, imagining that they are actual shoppers. You'll soon get a real handle on the process, and if you're a developer, your client will certainly appreciate the added insight you have into the Magento ordering process. This is incredibly important to your client, so it should be important to you!

For this section, I have placed two sample orders to use for our journey through the **backend order process**. Logging into the Magento backend, we can see our latest orders listed in the left sidebar of the **Dashboard**:

Last 5 Orders		
Customer	Items	Grand Total
Bret Williams	2	$6,110.47
Bret Williams	1	$437.14

From here we can click on the order that we wish to process, or we can go to **Sales | Orders** in the top navigation bar and then select the order from the list of all orders. Either way, we end up with a detailed view of the order.

Let's take each section of this screen separately and explain what each contributes to the ordering process.

Order # 100000001 (the order confirmation email was sent)		Account Information	
Order Date	Sep 6, 2011 2:03:09 AM	Customer Name	**Bret Williams**
Order Status	Pending	Email	support@novusweb.com
Purchased From	**Main Website** **Main Store** **English**	Customer Group	**NOT LOGGED IN**
Placed from IP	76.176.44.83		

The first section, shown on the left-hand side, summarizes key order information, including the timestamp of the order (date and time), the current status (which by default is *pending*), from which Magento store the purchase was made, and the customer's IP. The IP number could be important if the customer makes a fraudulent purchase. Your merchant bank and law enforcement agencies can use this to track down suspected thieves.

New orders, by default, are marked as **Pending**. This means the order is awaiting your attention. The customer has already been charged and has received an e-mail confirmation of their order, but it's now up to you to complete the order, eventually taking it to a stage of *complete*.

The box on the right-hand side tells us the name of the customer, their e-mail address, and the fact that they checked out without registering (more on customer groups later in this chapter).

The next row of boxes shows the billing and shipping addresses of the purchaser. Notice that these are *editable*. Sometimes a customer, upon receiving their e-mail receipt, will see that they made an error in either one or both of these. If the customer contacts you with corrected information, you can easily make the changes here.

The third row of boxes gives you information about the payment method and the buyer's choice of shipping for the order.

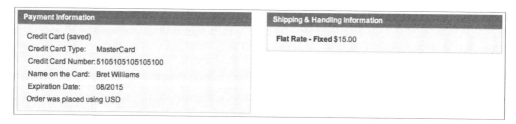

 Note that when using the sample data configuration, you are allowed to take and store credit card numbers in Magento. For **PCI Compliance**, this is a big no-no. Once you set up your payment gateways (later in this chapter), you won't see credit card numbers anywhere in Magento. And that's a good thing! You do not want to take on the liability of protecting your customer's credit card information from unscrupulous hackers and, sometimes, even employees.

On row four, you'll find the list of products ordered by the customer, the amount charged, and the amount of sales tax applicable for each line item.

In the previous screenshot, you'll see that the **Item Status** is **Partial**. In preparation for this example order, I reduced the available inventory for this item to "1" and allowed for backorders. While one of the missing pieces on this screen is the ability to see exactly what the inventory for a line item is, you are alerted that this product is not completely in stock.

The final row of boxes are quite interesting and important. First, on the left-hand side in the following screenshot, is how you can keep notes on an order and update the customer. Let's say, as in this case, that you have discovered that you only have one remaining chair and that more chairs won't arrive for another two weeks. By filling in this information here, and checking the **Notify Customer by E-mail** box, you can update the customer (*Would you like us to hold your order, or cancel it?*) and have the update sent automatically to the buyer. Furthermore, by checking the **Visible on Frontend** box, the customer—if they are registered (and this sample customer is not)—can view the update in the **Account Information** section of your store.

All comments entered will be appended to the list at the bottom of the box.

The box on the right-hand side is the transaction summary of the order.

For the second sample order, there are two differences that I wanted to illustrate. The first was how a **configurable product** is represented. In the next screenshot, you can see that I ordered a **Gaming Computer** with additional choices for such things as **Case**, **RAM**, and **Hard Drive**:

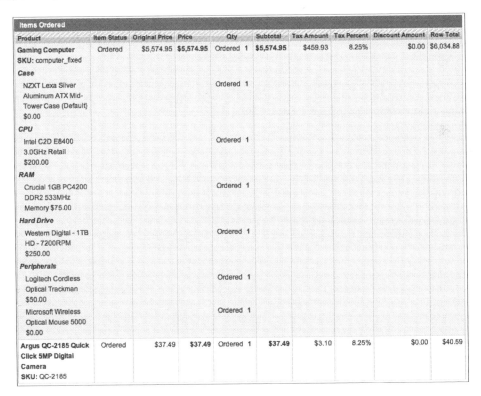

The second difference is that the **Item Status** is **Ordered**, as I paid by check or money order, as shown below. This means that as a purchaser, I will be sending payment to the retailer before the product is shipped.

Payment Information	Shipping & Handling Information
Check / Money order	Flat Rate - Fixed $35.00
Order was placed using USD	

Converting orders to invoices

The next step for you, as the person who is processing orders, is to **invoice** this order. In Magento, this means that you are confirming the order, and proceeding with processing.

 You can go straight to shipping for an order without having to generate an invoice. However, it is good practice to go from order to invoice to shipping. In this manner, you are tracking not only the products, but the payments, as well.

To convert an order into an invoice, click the button at the top of the page labeled **Invoice**. The resulting page is similar to the order page, except that it allows you to perform certain additional functions, as follows:

- **Create shipment**. In the box titled **Shipping Information**, you can check the box labeled **Create Shipment** and add any tracking numbers to the invoice.

- **Change the quantity of products to invoice**. As in our first example, if you have fewer products in stock than actually on hand, you may want to alter the number of products you are invoicing. Any remaining products will cause the order to remain open for future invoicing.

- **Add comments**. As on the order page, you can add a comment to the invoice and select whether the comment should be appended to the invoice. Otherwise, the comment will be added to the order history.

Once you have made any of the changes specified here, you can click on **Submit Invoice**, which will convert the order to an invoice, and record the order as an actual sale. This is key, as your analysis of sales for your store rely on the analysis of invoices, not orders. If you have not shipped the items yet, the status of the order is now shown as **Processing**.

Remember: *Orders are not sales.* Invoices are sales.

Once we have converted an order into an invoice, the box on the **Dashboard** screen titled **Lifetime Sales** is updated and shows the total sales for the chosen period, minus shipping and sales taxes, as shown in the following screenshot:

Creating shipments

Now that we have created our invoice, and once we have shipped the purchased products, we can create one or more shipments. To do this, open the order as before and click on the **Ship** button near the top of the screen.

On this screen, you can add **tracking numbers** for your shipments, as well as indicate the quantity of each product shipped. In the next screenshot, I have added a sample UPS tracking number. You can add as many as required (you may need to ship an order in more than one box, for instance).

Lower on the page, you will find each line item of the order with a field allowing you to change the number of products shipped, shown as follows:

Once you have made any changes, including adding any comments, you can click on **Submit Shipment**. If you ship all ordered items, the status of the order will change to **Complete**; otherwise, the order will remain in a **Processing** state.

The following example is a typical e-mail sent to the buyer, showing that the order has been shipped, and includes its tracking information:

Once you become familiar with the sales process, you'll have a much better understanding of how various system configurations affect how orders are moved through Magento.

Payment methods

In today's online retailing world, most purchasers use credit cards (or debit cards) for payment. Nothing new there. However, the process—of taking someone's credit card details online, verifying the card for available purchasing limit, drawing the amount for the purchase from the buyer's account, and transferring it into your bank account—is one that remains a mystery to many. Of all the components that comprise online commerce, the process of moving money—in this case from the credit card account of the buyer to your bank account—remains one of the most complex of all.

Without the ease of credit cards, online e-commerce might well have been growing at a much slower pace. However, the use of credit cards—and the potential for misuse—concerns your shoppers, particularly when the press reports stories of hackers breaking into retailer databases. What is important is that online purchases have never been "hacked". That is, no one has been prosecuted for stealing credit card information used to buy online as long as the store is using SSL encryption. To ease consumers' fears, several payment systems have evolved over the past decade, each designed to help you process the financial transactions for your store, while providing increased security and processes necessary to give both you and your buyer a safer and easier transaction process.

As a Magento administrator, you have within Magento several default payment systems available based on your own needs. Each one requires that the store owner enroll and qualify, but, having done so, allows the store to provide buyers with a convenient, secure means of paying for their purchase.

In this section, we will cover the most common, popular payment systems and how they work with Magento. This is intended to familiarize you with how each system interacts with Magento—the buyer and the store owner. Once you understand how they work, you will be able to appropriately decide on which system(s) you want to employ, which also makes configuring Magento that much easier.

Classes of payment systems

The determination of which payment system to utilize in your Magento store is driven by a comparison of pros and cons (isn't everything in life?). In terms of credit card sales, there are two basic classifications of **payment systems**: *off-site* and *on-site*.

Off-site payment systems

Off-site systems allow buyers to make purchase choices, but pay for their order on another website which offers the buyer a sense of greater security and fraud protection. The buyer is actually paying the off-site payment provider, who in turn pays the store owner once there is sufficient verification that the order has been processed and shipped. Each system has different degrees of verification based on the type of products sold, the history of the merchant (that is, have there been previous problems with the merchant's reliability?), and the amount of the purchase.

The pros of using this system are as follows:

- Provides extra layers of protection to buyers against unscrupulous merchants.
- Quick merchant approval. No credit report is required.
- No PCI compliance requirements.

- Easy integration into almost any e-commerce platform.

Many buyers like these systems because of the added layer of protection against merchants who fail to deliver the expected results.

Additionally, the off-site system qualifies the merchant as opposed to a merchant account provider or bank. For first-time e-commerce merchants, this qualification is usually easier to obtain, as no credit report is required.

The downsides to these types of payment systems are as follows:

- Takes buyers off your e-commerce site
- May require the buyer to enroll in a third-party payment system
- The merchant has limited access to buyer information, including e-mail addresses

The dominant off-site systems are **PayPal Express**, **PayPal Standard**, and **Google Checkout**.

On-site payment systems

Almost any well-developed e-commerce store will allow buyers to pay directly on the site without having to go off-site to another payment system. While most will also provide off-site payment alternatives, by providing an on-site payment process, the merchant eliminates any reluctance the buyer may have to enroll in a third-party payment system.

The advantages of on-site payment systems are as follows:

- Keeps the buyer on the site, exposed to the merchant's own available merchandise
- Eliminates the need for a buyer to register or enroll with an outside payment system
- Gives the merchant access to all buyer information for follow-up, processing, and future marketing

In order to succeed with on-site payment systems, merchants need to consider design elements and payment system brands that will help buyers have confidence in the security of the payment process. Most buyers have no history with new merchants; therefore, merchants, if they wish to offer on-site payments, should pay special attention to methods of communicating the security of the buyer's information.

The cons of using on-site payment systems include the following:

- Requires a merchant banking account, which can be difficult to obtain for new businesses
- Site may be subject to PCI Compliance
- Integration with e-commerce platforms is more complex

On-site payments are processed through gateways. **Gateways** accept the customer payment information, as well as the order total, by means of a secure connection between your store server and the gateway's servers. The gateway validates the buyer's information and returns a result of success or error, which your store platform processes accordingly.

Currently, the most popular payment gateways include **Authorize.net**, **Moneybookers**, and **PayPal Pro**.

PayPal

In the early, heady days of e-commerce, many merchants lacked an easy way to implement credit card processing, particularly with the lack of sophisticated platforms such as Magento. To accommodate the growing legion of online buyers, and to provide a form of third-party protection for both transaction partners, **PayPal** was created. By signing up for a PayPal account, the buyer could pay for purchases at participating merchants, the money would be withdrawn from the buyer's bank account or credit card, and the merchant would be paid, less a processing fee. Both were protected against fraud by PayPal.

Today, PayPal remains one of the most popular payment systems in the world because it does allow for global purchases. You can sell to buyers in other countries, as long as they have a PayPal account, knowing that you will receive payment. Most regular merchant accounts, such as those used by brick and mortar retailers, restrict sales to only buyers with cards issued by US banks.

The downside to using PayPal used to be that buyers would have to sign up for PayPal if you, the merchant, offered it as a payment system. That changed some years ago: today your buyers don't have to sign up for PayPal. They can purchase using a credit card without enrolling. However, you as the merchant have to pay higher fees than a regular merchant account, and PayPal does everything it can to encourage enrollment, which may be a turnoff to some shoppers.

If you are considering PayPal as a payment system, the store owner must enroll with PayPal and choose one of three variations:

- **PayPal Express**: This is the simplest and fastest way to implement PayPal. In essence, your store's **Add to Cart** buttons become links directly to PayPal. Items are placed into a PayPal shopping cart, not yours, and the buyer must return to your store after each selection. It is the least integrated method, meaning that it does not provide your users with a consistent shopping experience.

- **PayPal Standard**: This is perhaps the best implementations of PayPal. It provides PayPal subscribers with the ease of buying with their PayPal account, and also allows others to use their own credit card without enrolling in PayPal; and it does not come into play until the shopper has completed all other steps on your checkout page. Instead of creating the shopping cart on PayPal, as with PayPal Express, the shopper creates the cart within Magento and then goes to PayPal only during the step of final payment. This gives the store owner greater access to information about their shoppers (for example, abandoned carts), and retains much more of the intended brand experience that you intended.

- **PayPal Pro**: Consider this an alternative to Authorize.net, which we will discuss a bit later. Shoppers enter credit card information right on your site, never being taken to PayPal. PayPal users cannot use their PayPal account, although you can use one of the other methods in conjunction with PayPal Pro. The downside is that the store owner must qualify in the same manner as if they were applying for a regular merchant account. Furthermore, your Magento installation is subject to PCI compliance scans.

PayPal is well integrated into Magento. It's no surprise, since eBay, the owner of PayPal, purchased Magento in 2011. In fact, it's quite evident that Magento would like store owners to consider using PayPal, as shown by the emphasis of PayPal in the system configuration sidebar menu, which you can see as follows:

Authorize.Net

Owned by CyberSource, **Authorize.Net** is the most popular payment gateway in the United States and Canada. In Magento, you have the opportunity to configure your store to use two different versions of Authorize.net's gateway:

- **Authorize.Net AIM**. Labeled simply Authorize.Net in the Payment Methods configuration section, AIM stands for Advanced Integration Method. AIM is an on-site payment system.

- **Authorize.Net Direct Post**. This is a fairly new service for Authorize. net. Direct Post works very similarly to PayPal Standard, in that once the customer is ready to complete their order, they are taken to the Authorize.Net website to enter their credit card information. Unlike PayPal, you still need a merchant account in order to use Direct Post.

Google Checkout

The behemoth that we call Google started offering payment services to merchants some years ago, perceived as a competitor to PayPal. Like PayPal, buyers can register with Google Checkout to store credit card and address information. As with PayPal, participating merchants allow buyers to use their Google accounts to buy products without having to disclose payment information to the merchant.

Google Checkout is an off-site payment system. Buyers who choose Google Checkout are taken to Google as the final step in the checkout process where they log in and verify their purchase.

The big difference between Google Checkout and PayPal Standard—the PayPal method most like Google Checkout—is how the merchant interacts with Google. Google places more responsibility on the merchant in terms of configurations for shipping and sales taxes, and in how they update Google when items ship or orders are canceled. Merchants do have to go through a slightly more complex verification process, as well.

MoneyBookers

For merchants selling internationally, and who want an on-site solution, Magento includes integration with MoneyBookers. **MoneyBookers** is not as well known in the US; but globally, it is the most popular payment processing gateway. The more impressive aspect of MoneyBookers is how complex the system must be to accommodate all the variations of their gateway based on location. As you can see from this next screenshot, there are different configurations required based on the countries in which the merchant wants to sell:

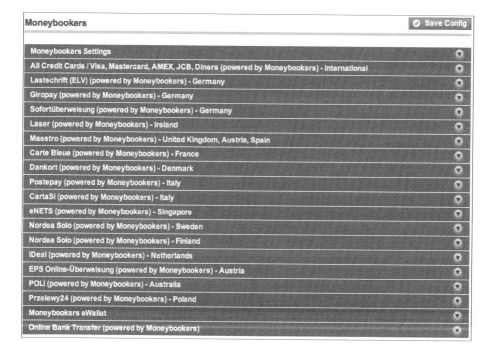

How Magento integrates payment systems

One of the more enjoyable aspects of Magento is that developers have gone to great lengths to integrate each of their default payment systems as fully as possible into Magento. That means that for each off-site system, where possible, the buyer is returned to your site after completing their off-site payment and the order information is sent back to your Magento store so that you can manage the order in the backend just as with any on-site purchase.

Additionally, Magento includes links within each payment system configuration to give you the information that you need to complete the configuration process. The more important concern—and the purpose of this section—is to understand the various alternatives and consult with the store owner to determine which one(s) to configure. There are no right and wrong answers; it's a matter of merchant ability and preference, and customer expectations and needs.

Shipping methods

Magento includes, by default, integrations with the most popular shipping carriers: **UPS, USPS (United States Postal Service), FedEx,** and **DHL** (no longer shipping in the US, DHL is available in other countries). As with the payment methods, all but UPS require that you establish a customer account with each carrier in order to complete your configuration.

In addition to the common carriers, merchants can simply offer flat rate shipping costs or set up a table of rates based on weight, price, or number of items ordered. Merchants can also provide a site-wide free shipping condition, based on a minimum order amount.

Let's now explore some of the more complex configuration issues relating to shipping.

Common configuration choices

Every shipping method configuration shares some common configuration choices:

- **Enabled**: If you want the particular shipping method available at the Website level and below (that is, all Store Views), select **Yes**.

- **Title**: You may want to use a name that is more recognizable by your customers, or is translated for a different language Store View.

- **Ship to applicable countries**: You can choose to offer a particular method to all allowed countries, as defined under **System | Configuration | General | General**, or only to countries which you select in the field just below.

- **Sort order**: By entering numbers into these fields, you can control the order in which various enabled shipping methods are listed on the store checkout page.

- **Calculate handling fee**: If you wish to add an additional **handling fee** to the fixed shipping cost, you can do so by adding a fixed per order fee or one calculated as a percentage of the total product prices. Handling fees are not shown separately, but are added into whatever shipping costs are displayed to the buyer.

Flat rate shipping

This is perhaps the most straight-forward shipping configuration as it involves the fewest configuration choices. The more important ones is **Type**. You can charge a fixed shipping cost on a per-order or per-item basis. For instance, you might charge $5.00 for shipping any order of any size, or you might change $2.50 shipping on every item in the order.

Table rates

Setting up a rate table for shipping is by far the most complex of all shipping method configurations, as it requires that you prepare your shipping rate table separately, saving it as a CSV file, then importing it into Magento at the Website level.

The key to successfully implementing a rate table is to click on the **Export CSV** button (you must be at a Website level in the **Current Configuration Scope**). Open the downloaded file in a spreadsheet program or text editor and enter in your desired values according the columns shown in the file. Given next is a portion of a spreadsheet with rates entered according to the column names at the top:

	A	B	C	D	E
1	Country	Region/State	Zip/Postal Code	Weight (and above)	Shipping Price
2	US	*	*	0	5
3	US	*	*	10	15
4	US	*	*	25	30
5	US	AK	*	0	10
6	US	AK	*	10	25
7	US	AK	*	25	50
8	US	HI	*	0	10
9	US	HI	*	10	25
10	US	HI	*	25	50

Let's go over each column and explain what should be entered in each:

- **Country**: Enter the two-letter abbreviation of the country for which the rate applies. An asterisk (*) means that the rate applies to all allowed countries.

- **Region/State**: Use the two-letter code for the state or region of the country. In the case of US states, an asterisk means the rate applies to the "lower 48", the states except for Alaska and Hawaii. Since it commonly costs more to ship to these states, Magento wisely makes a provision for setting rates only for the continental US without having to list each state separately. If you intend to ship to Alaska and Hawaii, you will need to include line items for each, as shown in the table.

- **Zip/Postal Code**: Usually, you would include all codes within a given state or region. However, you can be quite granular by entering specific postal codes in this column.
- **Weight (and above)**: Table rates work by taking the total weight of the products in the order. Use this column to provide different shipping rates based on this weight total.
- **Shipping Price**: This is the rate that will be applied to the order.

The previous chart shows the columns for *weight-based* calculations. For *price-based* or *quantity-based* calculations, the Weight column is named differently to reflect these alternatives. You can choose either of these alternatives using the drop-down menu called **Condition** in the **Table Rates** panel.

Once you have your table rates set, use the **Import** configuration function to upload your CSV file to Magento.

Free shipping

All the common carrier methods allow you to set one method (for example, ground, overnight) as a free method based on a minimum order amount. The **Free Shipping** method gives you the global ability to offer free shipping based on a minimum order amount, as well. The difference is that with the **Free Shipping** method, you cannot specify or display a particular method such as ground, overnight, and so on.

Generally, you would use this method in conjunction with the **Flat Rate** or **Table Rate** methods. If you're now asking, "why not just specify no shipping cost in your table rate CSV file?", here's one scenario where you would still find value in using Free Shipping with a Table Rate configuration.

Let's say you've set up your Table Rates to charge based on weight. The heavier the order, the more the shipping costs, much like in our earlier example. However, for customers who order a total of $500 or more, you'd like to give them free shipping. Since your Table Rates are based on weight, the **Free Shipping** method gives you the opportunity to offer free shipping once your profit margin is sufficient.

Configuring sales tax rules

As you know, when selling products to consumers, you may need to charge and collect sales tax. Some states don't require sales tax, but most due. Moreover, the rules for calculating and collecting sales tax varies from state to state, country to country.

Before configuring your Sales Tax Rules, you may need to consult with your accountant. The examples in this book are purposely simple; your actual sales tax configuration may be more complex depending on your situation.

Before we dive into creating Sales Tax Rules, let's understand a bit about the relationship Magento creates between Sales Tax Rules, Customer Tax Classes, Product Tax Classes, and Tax Rates & Zones. The following chart illustrates this relationship:

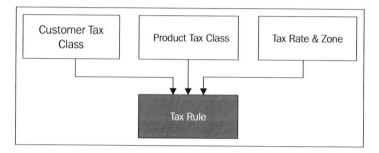

The tax rule that calculates sales tax on any particular item is based on a combination of the type of customer, the type of product and the applicable tax rate based on the geographic location of the shipping destination.

Creating a sales tax rate

As an example, let's assume you're located in Massachusetts. Since your physical location is in the Bay State, you're obligated to charge customers a 6.25% tax on all applicable purchases (again, *please* consult your accountant for advice; the tax rates used in this example are for illustrative purposes only).

Therefore, to create the appropriate Sales Tax Rate:

1. Go to **Sales | Tax | Manage Tax Zones & Rates** in your Administrative backend.
2. Click on **Add New Tax Rate** near the top-right of your screen.
3. For **Tax Identifier**, enter a value that is descriptive of the rule. In this case, we'll use **MA Sales Tax.**
4. Of course, choose **Massachusetts** as the **State** in the drop-down menu.
5. Since your tax will apply to all zip codes, leave **Zip/Post is Range** set to **No.**
6. Enter **6.25** as the **Rate Percent.**

7. Finally, if you wish to use a name other than the **Tax Identifier** for any of your **Store Views**, enter it in the **Tax Titles** section.

8. Click on **Save Rate** to save your changes.

Creating the sales tax rule

Creating the Sales Tax Rate doesn't yet mean that purchases by customers in Massachusetts will have a tax levied. Referring to the previous diagram, you now must combine the **Tax Rate** with a **Customer Tax Class** and a **Product Tax Class**.

1. Go to **Sales | Tax | Manage Tax Rules**.

2. Click on **Add New Tax Rule**.

3. On this screen, as shown in the next screenshot, you combine the various components that together create the **Sales Tax Rule**:

4. Enter a descriptive name in the **Name** field, such as *MA-Retail-Taxable*.

5. To continue our example, click and select **Retail Customer**, **Taxable Goods**, and **MA Sales Tax** in the fields shown.

6. Click on **Save Rule**.

Now, whenever a retail customer purchases a taxable product to be shipped to a Massachusetts address, 6.25% sales tax will be added to the price of the product.

> **Charging tax on shipping**
>
> In most cases, you will not be charging sales tax for shipping costs. However, if you are required to do so, you would designate that requirement in the **Shipping Methods** configurations.

Outgoing e-mails

In past years, one of the banes of using Magento was customizing outgoing e-mails sent to your customers for orders, invoices, site registrations, and so on. It was truly a painful experience.

With Magento today, administrators have it much, much easier. You can quickly and easily create multiple versions of e-mails with different styles and content. Let's go through the process of creating an alternative version of the order confirmation e-mail and assigning it to one of our Stores.

1. Go to **System | Transactional E-mails** in your Magento backend. Although you'll see an empty list, this screen only shows customized e-mails once they are created.

2. Click on **Add New Template**.

3. The first step in the process is to select an existing Magento e-mail as a template for your new e-mail. Let's select **New Order** and click on **Load Template**.

4. You'll see that **Used as Default For** shows you where in the system configuration this particular e-mail is assigned. In this case as the **New Order Confirmation Template** for all Websites and Store Views, although any Website or Store View can override this by assigning a new e-mail template as we will do in this example.

5. Fill in an applicable name for your new e-mail in the **Template Name** field. We'll use *Electronics New Order*, since we're going to use this new e-mail for our Electronics Store.

6. In most cases, and until you become more familiar with Magento variables, you're not likely to need to change the **Template Subject** field. That said, you may want to include something like *Thank You* before the shown content.

There are several variables that you can use in an e-mail template. If you find one which you wish to use in the subject, add it to the **Template Content** field, then cut and paste it into the **Template Subject** field.

Before we continue with the e-mail editing process, let's talk about **designing e-mails**. E-mails which are constructed poorly or improperly will most often times end up in the recipients spam filter or, at best, be unreadable by their e-mail program. If you're not familiar with designing e-mails that get past spam filters and look good to recipients, go online and look for recent articles regarding HTML e-mail design. While this is a topic which deserves much more space and attention than what we can provide here, in general HTML e-mails should be table-based. I know, everyone wants table-less web pages, but e-mail's different. CSS styling should be inline; never as a separate file or stuffed into the header area. You should also pay attention to width, as most e-mail readers—especially those on smart phones—have limited viewing widths.

For now, use the Magento templates as a guide and if you know your way around HTML, you'll easily find ways of modifying the template to your liking without breaking anything. For our example:

1. Scroll to the bottom of the **Template Content** field and find the HTML that contains **Thank you**. Add, before the `</p>` tag, *(space)We hope to see you back again very soon!* This line should look something like this:

```
<td bgcolor="#EAEAEA"
    align="center"
    style="background:#EAEAEA; text-align:center;">
  <center><p style="font-size:12px; margin:0;">
    Thank you, <strong>{{var store.getFrontendName()}}</strong>
    We hope to see you back again very soon!</p>
  </center>
</td>
```

2. The **Template Styles** field contains the only CSS styling not set as an inline style. Here you can change the overall, default values for the body and other elements. For this example, we're going to change our body color value to `#990000` just to illustrate this change. This will set the text color of the e-mail to red.

3. Click on **Preview Template** to view your changes. In this example, our changes are shown in the following screenshot:

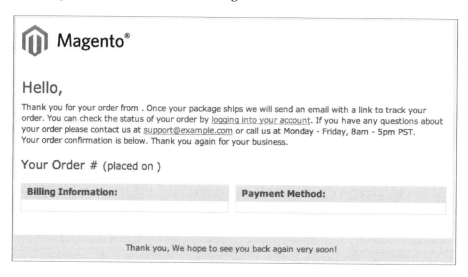

While the change in text color may not be evident, you can see that the bottom thank you line has changed. What is not shown in this preview are some of the dynamic values, such as the name of the Store, which is supposed to appear right after **Thank you**.

4. Click on **Save Template** to save your work.

While it may seem a bit tedious, if you need distinct differences in the e-mails sent by your different **Stores**, Magento does give you tremendous flexibility to craft your e-mails to suit your brand and purpose.

Now that we have created a unique e-mail for our Electronics Store, we need to assign it for use in that store.

1. Go to **System | Configuration | Sales | Sales E-mails**.

2. Change your **Current Configuration Scope** to **Electronics/English**.

3. Open the center panel titled **Order**.

4. De-select the checkbox to the right-hand side of **New Order Confirmation Template**. This will activate the drop-down for you to change.

5. Select **Electronics New Order** from the drop-down menu.

6. To save your new configuration, click on **Save Config**.

From now on, when a customer orders from the Electronics Store, they will receive the new, customized e-mail we created in this example.

Changing address formats

Customer addresses, as you can imagine, are formatted differently in different countries of the world. Fortunately, you can set the format of addresses for a given Store View by going to **System | Configuration | Customer | Address Templates**. The format will be the same for all customers in the given store, but if your Store Views are language/region specific, this can help you provide proper formatting for your customer e-mails.

Summary

Magento is, above all things, a selling tool, a means of presenting products, taking orders and payments, and managing the fulfillment of those orders. Even though there are common steps to ordering online, Magento provides one of the most comprehensive and versatile ordering mechanisms to consumers among open source platforms. If nothing else, this chapter has demonstrated the impressive scope of its functionality.

As you begin to move closer to launching your new Magento store, you will re-visit the various configurations and processes relating to the sales cycle. Don't be discouraged by this. In fact, I find that as I discover more of Magento's power, I am empowered to create more ways of promoting and selling to customers.

In this chapter, we:

- Learned about the Magento sales process
- Went through a typical order management process
- Examined the various payment systems available in a default Magento installation
- Explored shipping method configurations
- Created a sales tax rule
- Customized an outgoing e-mail

You should also keep in mind that there are over 4,000 extensions to Magento, many of which add additional functionality for all the areas we covered in this chapter. If Magento doesn't exactly provide what you need, chances are some third-party developer has created an add-on that meets your needs.

The next item on our agenda is to manage the various non-product content elements of a Magento store, which we'll cover in the next chapter.

6
Managing Non-product Content

As important as products and product information are to e-commerce, successful online stores need more in order to attract customers and fortify the store's brand. Even printed catalogs often contain information about the seller, including hours of operation, return policies, company history, and more. This **non-product content** is essential.

To gain an understanding of how to create and manipulate non-product content, we will:

- Review how Magento incorporates content
- Learn how to create content pages in your Magento store
- Create and use static blocks
- Utilize built-in content widgets
- Review the principles of layout customization

Once you know how to interweave non-product content throughout your online store, you will no doubt discover innovative ways to increase customer engagement.

The Magento content management system

As with most e-commerce platforms, Magento's management of **non-product content** lacks some of the more robust features of a dedicated **Content Management System** — or **CMS** — such as *WordPress*, *Business Catalyst*, or *Joomla*. However, to its credit, Magento does provide a versatile system that takes into account the possible need for unique content for each of your stores.

As you would expect, the backend area for the management of CMS functions in Magento is under the **CMS** menu. This area includes sections for managing pages, static blocks, widgets, and polls. We will cover the first three in this chapter, reserving polls for *Chapter 7, Marketing Tools*.

Before we dig into each of these items, it's important to recall our discussion about blocks in *Chapter 4, Designs and Themes*. Whether configuring a page, or placing a static block or widget, Magento builds the final results by assembling blocks of information.

Pages

The pages that we will use in the CMS are not actually complete pages as they lack controls for the overall template items of the header, navigation, and footer. These pages actually refer to the central content of a page — that which lies within the overall page template. Within this page, we can add text, images, static blocks, and widgets to give the page it's core content. As we will examine in this section, you can add some of the same code as you did in the `local.xml` file to even manipulate elements outside the core content area, including blocks within the header, navigation, and footer.

To begin, let's look at and alter a default page provided by the sample data installed into a new Magento store.

Go to **CMS | Pages** in the Magento backend. With the sample data installed, you should see a list of pages, much like those shown in the following screenshot:

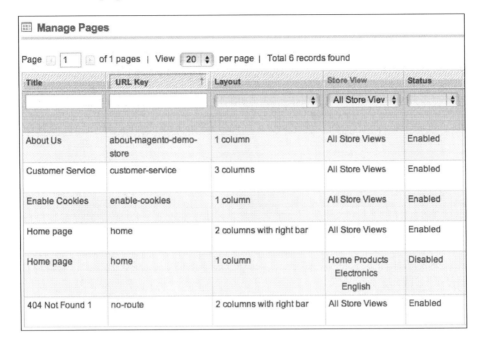

 There are two pages on this list that you should always keep available: **Enable Cookies** and **404 Not Found 1**. These pages are used by Magento to display error messages to visitors if they do not have cookies enabled in their browser or they reach a page that does not exist, respectively. You can always modify the content of these pages to suit your need, or even duplicate and modify them for different stores, but each store should have both of these pages enabled and assigned.

Customizing a CMS page

The first place that most designers want to begin modifying a store's design is the home page. The sample data installation installs two versions of the home page, one enabled for all stores, the other disabled and assigned to only one store. Both are created based on the base package layout and design.

As we discussed in *Chapter 4, Designs and Themes*, we don't ever want to modify the base package. If we really liked the design, we could duplicate the **layout** and **skin** files, place them within another package, such as the default package, and modify them there. However, 99.9% of the time you understandably don't want your new store looking like the Magento default.

So, let's begin our quest by assigning one of the other default themes installed in Magento and modify the resulting home page according to our tastes. By following this example process, you'll learn a lot about how page modifications work.

 Before doing any design modifications on a site, it's a good idea to turn off the caches. Go to **System | Cache Management** and select all the various cache types, and disable them. This way you won't have to continually refresh the cache after each change. Once you're finished updating your design, you can return and enable the caches again. If you have enabled compilation on your site, you should also disable it.

Assigning a theme

First, let's set our store to use the *modern theme*. It's a nice, simple store design that's not bad looking and easier on the eyes.

1. Go to **System | Configuration | General | Design** in the Magento backend.
2. For now, our changes will effect all the stores, so leave your **Current Configuration Scope** set to *Default*.
3. In the center panel, enter the following attributes:
   - **Templates**: *modern*
   - **Skin (Images / CSS)**: *modern*
   - **Layout**: *modern*
4. Click on **Save Config**.

If we now take a look at our home page, we should see something like the following screenshot :

Kind of messy, eh? Basically, it's because the home page is configured in the CMS to display certain elements that have not been styled or appropriately sized for this theme. Remember, the Magento **Fallback Method** says that if an element does not exist within the designated theme, Magento looks to the **default theme** of the **design package**, then into the **Base Package**. Many of the components that make up this page are not part of the *modern theme* and exist only in the **Base Package**.

Modifying the home page layout

Fortunately for us, the sample data installation provides an alternative home page that works very well with the modern theme:

1. Go to **CMS | Pages**.
2. Click on the first **home page** listed (with the **2 columns with right bar** layout).
3. Change the **Status** to *Disabled* and click on **Save**.
4. Now, click on the second **home page** listed (with the **1 column** layout).
5. Select **English, French,** and **German** as the store views under **Main Website** in the **Store View** list.
6. Change the **Status** to *Enabled* and click on **Save**.

Now look at your home page:

Much better. However, it does lack some of the dynamic elements which we might want on this page, such as a list of product categories, recently viewed products, and a summary of a visitor's shopping cart.

Return to your Magento backend, and if you're not there, go to **CMS | Pages**. Click on the active **home page** item and let's take a closer look at what dictates what is on this page.

First, we need to understand that pages created in the Magento CMS primarily dictate what appears in the content section of the page. This is the area highlighted in the next screenshot, apart from the header, top navigation, and footer regions:

As we'll see however, we can add XML statements to a page's design to manipulate other non-content areas of the page.

Remember the local.xml file

In *Chapter 4, Designs and Themes*, we introduced a new feature of Magento: the `local.xml` file. By using various XML handles, you can manipulate an entire template for all pages. The same principles apply when working with pages, although your changes here will only affect the edited page.

On the **Page Information** panel of the **Edit Page** screen, you should see the following menu:

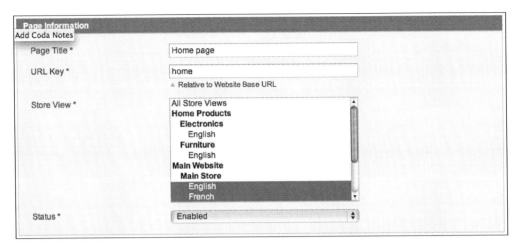

- **Page Title** is the title that will appear in the top of your browser, as well as the default name of any link you create to this page.

- **URL Key** is how the page is accessed in a URL path. For example, this page is accessible by going to `http://www.storedomain.com/home.html`. Magento assumes that your home page will have a URL Key of *home*. You should not change this unless you know what you're doing.

- **Store View** allows you to select which stores your page is applicable for. When you save your page, Magento does check to make sure another page with the same URL Key has not already been assigned to the same stores.

- **Status**, of course, indicates whether the page is active or not.

The Content screen

In the left-hand side tab, click on **Content**. This is the screen where you can add text, images, or dynamic content that will appear in the central content area of your page. You're also free to use HTML code, if you wish.

If you notice in the next screenshot, this sample data home page contains a **block reference**:

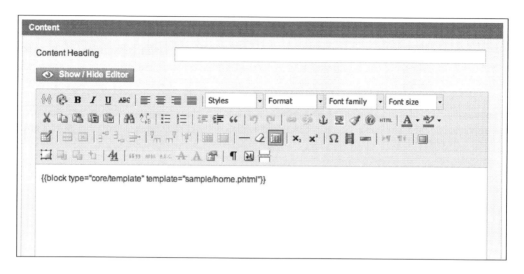

Just as we use blocks in the XML files that define our page layouts, we can also use them in this content area. However, the format is a bit different: instead of using XML, we use "handle bars" to denote dynamic code:

```
{{block type="core/template" template="sample/home.phtml"}}
```

This example tells Magento to include the content of an HTML page that we created and stored within a folder called `sample`. This folder lies within the directory of our theme (in this case, `modern`). This file, `home.phtml`, contains the HTML code to display the graphics showing on the home page, as shown earlier.

For our exercise, let's remove this code and replace it with the following:

Welcome to our store. We hope you enjoy shopping with us.

In the field at the top, labeled **Content Heading**, enter: *We'll beat any price.*

Click on **Save and Continue Edit** (this will let you remain on this screen) and open your home page in another browser window or tab. It should look something like the following screenshot:

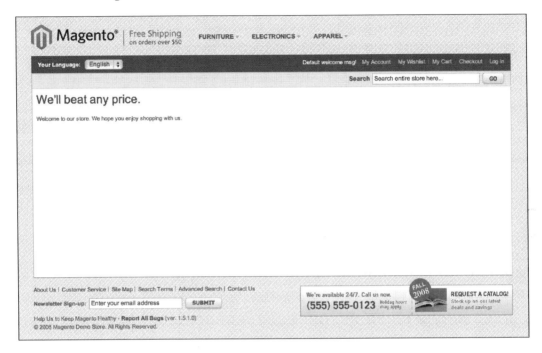

The text you put into the **Content Heading** field appears at the top of the content section automatically styled with an <h1> tag.

Now you've created your first custom home page content, but even you have to admit, it's not very engaging. Let's return to the **Edit Page** screen.

Adding variable content

At the upper right-hand side of the WYSIWYG bar at the top of the editing area of the panel, the first icon is for inserting dynamic information into your content. If you click on this icon, a pop-up dialog box will appear allowing you to select from several items, as shown in the following screenshot:

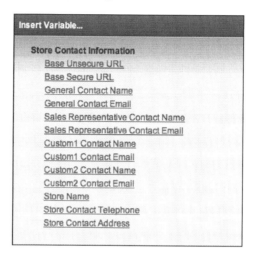

These variables can come in handy! For instance, if you're using the same home page layout for several stores, but want to show the name of the store in the content, click on **store name** in this list and a variable will be placed into the content editing field. This variable will show the name of the store as you configured it in the store management screen (**System | Manage Stores**). This is much easier than building multiple home pages, one for each store, just to show the current store name.

 You can create your own custom variables to use by going to **System | Custom Variables**. I use this feature to create custom variables for displaying a store's phone number or business hours.

The design screen

Before we put more content into the **Content** panel, click on the **Design** tab on the left-hand side. The design screen allows you to do much more in terms of altering the layout and surrounding elements of a page. As I suggested before, you can apply the same principles as you did with the `local.xml` file described in *Chapter 4, Designs and Themes* at the individual page level. These changes command the highest control over your page, overriding layout handles in the theme layout and `local.xml` files.

The next screenshot depicts the **Page Layout** panel for the same home page that we're using in this section:

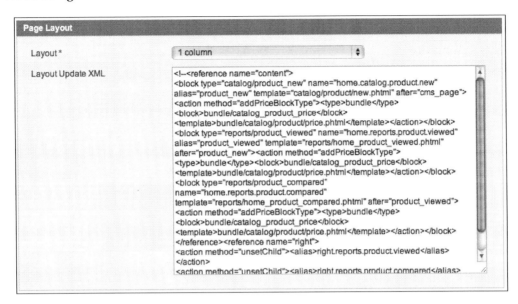

Every theme automatically includes four basic layouts:

- 1 column
- 2 columns with left sidebar
- 2 columns with right sidebar
- 3 columns

You also have the choice of selecting *Empty* in the **Layout** drop-down menu. This renders a page with nothing but what is directly specified in this page: no header, navigation, or footer. Go ahead and give it a try; I know you want to!

As for the layouts listed here, let's try each one and see how it immediately affects our page. Since we're already using the *1 column* layout, we'll start with *2 columns with left sidebar*:

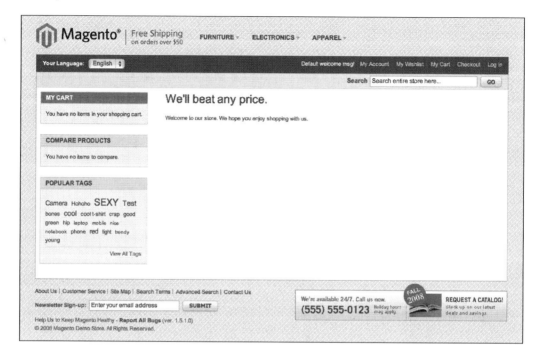

The elements, or blocks, showing in the left-hand sidebar are defined by the page layout XML file within the theme.

Compare this with the 2 *columns with right sidebar* layout:

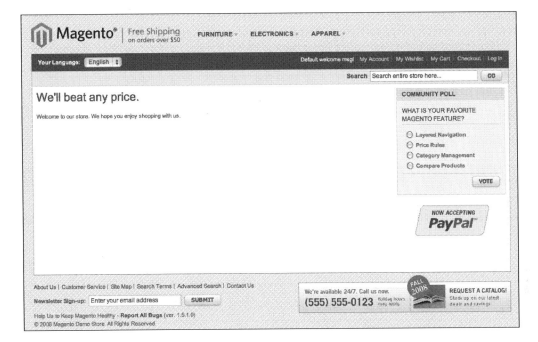

And finally, let's see what the 3 *columns* layout looks like:

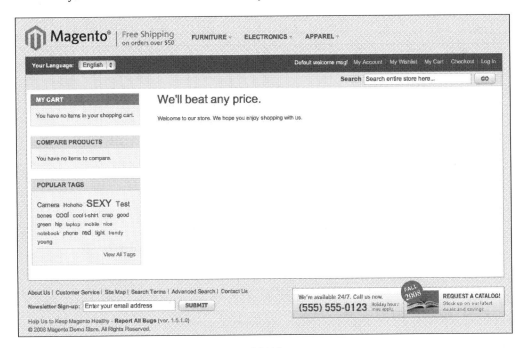

Wait a minute! This looks just like *2 columns with left sidebar*, right? Yes, because the template HTML file, `template/page/3columns.phtml`, used for this layout has the right sidebar commented out:

```php
<?php /*<div class="col-wrapper">*/ ?>
    <div class="col-main">
      <?php echo $this->getChildHtml('global_messages') ?>
      <?php echo $this->getChildHtml('content') ?>
    </div>
    <div class="col-left sidebar">
      <?php echo $this->getChildHtml('left') ?></div>
    </div>
    <?php /*<div class="col-right sidebar">
    <?php echo $this->getChildHtml('right') ?></div>*/ ?>
    <?php /*</div>*/ ?>
```

To see what all three columns might look like, we need to *un*-comment this code so it now looks as follows:

```php
<div class="col-wrapper">
    <div class="col-main">
      <?php echo $this->getChildHtml('global_messages') ?>
      <?php echo $this->getChildHtml('content') ?>
    </div>
    <div class="col-left sidebar">
      <?php echo $this->getChildHtml('left') ?></div>
</div>
<div class="col-right sidebar">
    <?php echo $this->getChildHtml('right') ?></div>
</div>
```

Now when we look at our home page, we see the following:

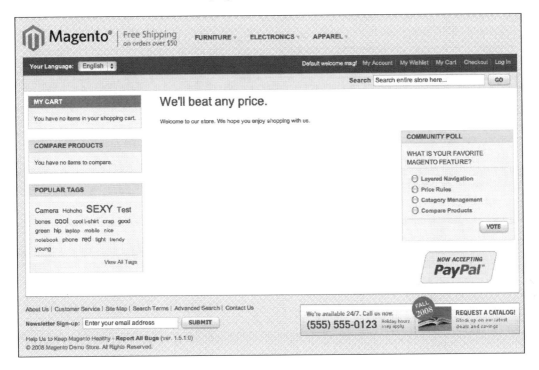

In the **Page Layout** panel, the larger field, called **Layout Update XML**, allows you to use XML code to manipulate the layout of the page. The sample code that's shown here is commented out (by using < - - before the code and - - > after the code), but remains to help you understand how to use XML to change the layout. Refer to *Chapter 4, Designs and Themes* for more information on using handles, blocks, and actions to manipulate page layouts.

The bottom panel on the design screen—**Custom Design**—allows you to set an alternative layout for the page that takes effect during the time span indicated in the two date fields.

The Meta Data screen

The final **Edit Page** screen is for adding meta keywords and a meta description for the page. Entering values here will override any default values that you set in the system configuration settings.

Static blocks

When managing a website, it's often nice to have snippets of code or design elements that you can use in one or more places, yet be able to edit without digging into the template files of your theme.

Static blocks allow you to do just that. From creating blocks for footer links to setting up a special promotional block, static blocks are styled in the same manner as you used in the **Edit Page Content** screen.

Once you create a static block, you can insert it into the **Content** panel of any page. You can also refer to a static block in a layout XML file. For example, the sample data installation includes a static block entitled *Footer Link*, with an identifier of *footer_links*. In the base package cms.xml layout file, this static block is referred to with the following code (the comments are included by default):

```
<reference name="footer">
  <block type="cms/block"
    name="cms_footer_links" before="footer_links">
  <!--
    The content of this block is taken from the database
      by its block_id.
    You can manage it in admin CMS -> Static Blocks
  -->
  <action method="setBlockId">
    <block_id>footer_links</block_id></action>
  </block>
</reference>
```

Once this block is defined, it can be called upon in a template HTML file, such as, in this case, footer.phtml, where the following PHP code pulls the *footer_links* static block content stored in the Magento database into this page component:

```
<?php echo $this->getChildHtml('cms_footer_links') ?>
```

Widgets

If you look at the WYSIWYG editor bar at the top of any content editing field, the second icon from the left is for inserting widgets into the content area. There are several types of widgets you can use in Magento.

While you can insert Widgets within any **Page Content** area, under **CMS | Widget**, you can configure widgets that will automatically appear on one or more pages in your store. It's a powerful way of adding customized features to your Magento store without doing a lot of heavy programming and configuration.

The next few sections are overviews of the default Magento widgets (some third-party extensions will add additional widgets). Whether you insert a widget into a **Page Content** area, or configure it to appear automatically, the configuration principles remain the same.

CMS page link widget

A **CMS page link widget** allows you to insert a link to one of your CMS pages. This is convenient if you have, for example, a page showing product brands that you want to insert into a static block or a CMS page.

As shown in the next screenshot, this widget gives you control over how the link will appear on your page. You can also choose between two layout templates, a **Block** style or an **Inline** style, depending on how you want the link to be controlled using CSS rules.

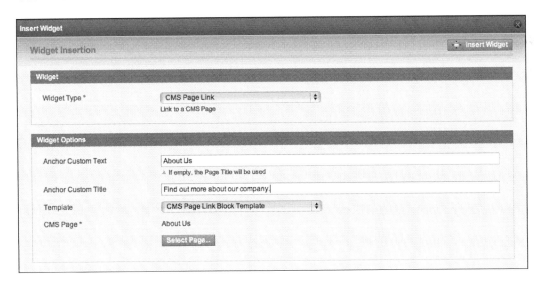

After saving the CMS page, the front end will show the link you specified, as shown in the following screenshot:

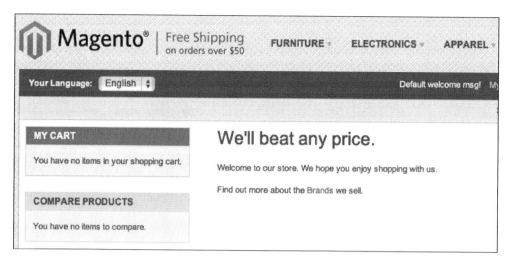

CMS static block

If you have static blocks that you have created, you can insert them into a page using the **CMS static block widget** instance. Simply choose the static block after clicking on **Select Block...** In the next screenshot, I added a static block that contained the cell phone image shown:

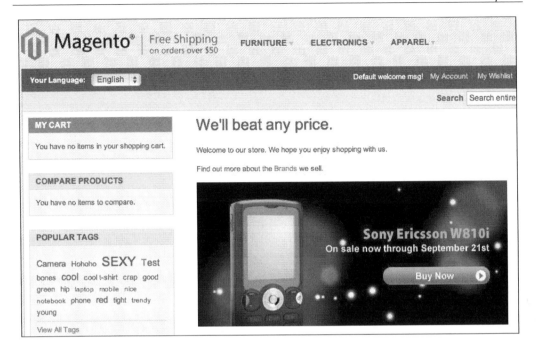

There is only one default template with a Magento installation. If you wish to change how static blocks are displayed in your theme, copy the template file from `app/design/frontend/base/default/template/cms/widget/static_block/default.phtml` and place it in the same directory hierarchy in your theme (for example, `app/design/frontend/[design package]/[design theme]/template/cms/widget/static_block/`). This might be handy if you want to add a new CSS style to your static block layouts Catalog a category link

The **catalog category link widget** gives you the ability to create custom links that will take the visitor to a list of all products within a designated category. You'll find the configuration choices described here apply to other similar widgets.

In the example shown next for instance, we have set up a widget to appear on all **Anchor Category** pages in the *Left Column* of the *English Language* **Store View**. Furthermore, we have chosen only three categories—**Cell Phones**, **Cameras**, and **Computers**—from the list of all categories. Once saved, this widget will automatically create a link only on those three category pages.

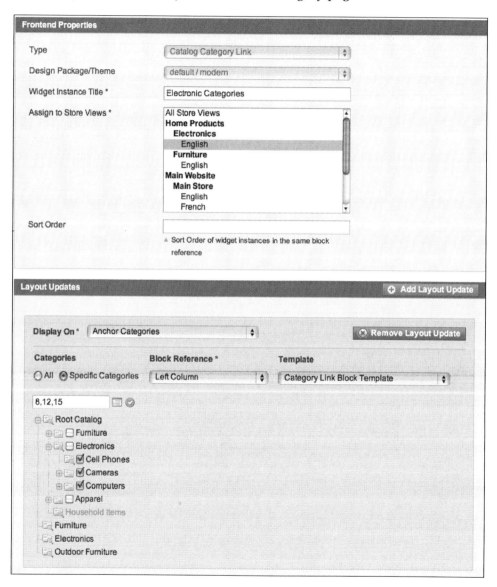

Now, if you click on the **Widget Options** tab on the left-hand side of the screen, you have the opportunity to name the link created by this widget, the link's title tag value, and select the **Category** page for the link destination, as shown in the following screenshot:

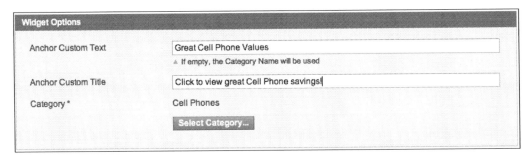

Using the values shown here, let's look now and see what this link looks like on one of our store pages:

In this example, you can see our new link appearing beneath the **POPULAR TAGS** block, with the title tag value we specified when a user hovers their mouse pointer over the link. By clicking on this link, the visitor is taken to the same category page as if they clicked on **Cell Phones** in the upper navigation panel on the page.

Creating a new products list

Some e-commerce platforms designate new products using a simple checkbox. While this may be quick, Magento approaches new products with its usual degree of increased functionality. To set a product as *new*, you simply enter a **Set Product as New from Date** and, optionally, a **Set Product as New to Date**, as shown in the following screenshot from the **General** tab of the **Product Information** screen:

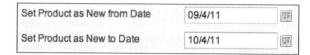

In this example, the edited product would be considered by Magento as *new* from September 4, 2012 through October 4, 2012. I like the ability to pre-determine when a **new product** would no longer be considered *new* without having to manually go through potentially hundreds or thousands of products and manually de-select a checkbox.

Set New When You Import

If you regularly import products from lists provided by distributors or manufacturers, many such feeds include a field that flags new products. When you import these products into Magento (see *Chapter 3, Managing Products*), you could set the **New from Date** field as the date of the import. You can either calculate the **New to Date** field (for example, add 30 days to the **New from Date** value), or leave it blank if you want the product to remain new for an indefinite period of time. This process keeps your new products changing, fresh, and up-to-date without continued interaction on your part.

Similar in setup to the aforementioned, the **Catalog New Products List Widget**, shown next, is likewise configured by setting the applicable store views, on what pages the widget is to appear, the desired block reference and, in this case, one of three display templates.

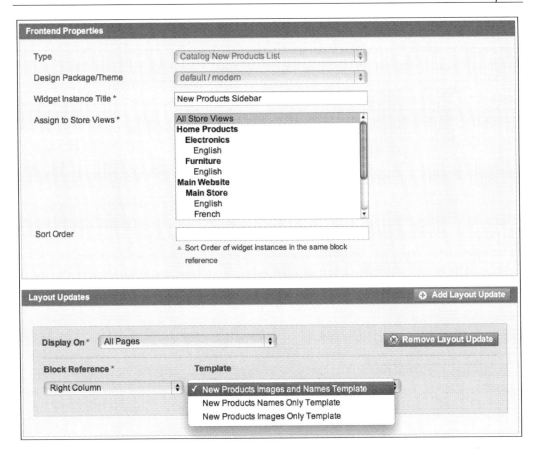

Catalog a product link

The **Catalog product link widget** works very much like the **catalog category link widget**, except, of course, you're choosing a specific **Product Detail Page** for the visitor instead of a **Category Page**.

Recently compared and recently viewed products

These two widgets do just as you would expect: display **Recently Compared** and **Recently Viewed** products in blocks you configure to appear in select pages in your store. Most Magento themes include these as sidebar blocks. However, I've found value in including these in such distinct locations as the Cart Page, the Checkout Page, and the Contact Us Page.

Principles of customizing layouts

After installing and configuring many Magento stores, I'm convinced that if you master the process of managing layouts, your stores will produce better sales results and give you better opportunities to customize a visitor's experience based on the needs of both the retailer and the customer.

That being said, the complexity of the Magento architecture demands your dedicated time and effort to achieve a level of true mastery. I suggest you carefully review *Chapter 4, Designs and Themes* and this chapter, truly examining the examples. As you do that, remember the following keys:

- At their core, page layouts are determined by XML files which specify the location of various blocks.

- Template files contain the HTML and PHP code that creates the final output of the pages.

- The graphic design of pages are greatly influenced by the CSS, JavaScript, and image files located in the `skin/` directory. By altering these, you can do quite a lot of brand customization.

- The Magento CMS functionality works best when you understand how blocks are used to build pages, even if you don't actually dig into the layout and template files.

- Above all, experiment. Especially with the CMS, you really can't break anything. The more you try different configurations, the more opportunities you'll discover to give your Magento store the added punch it deserves.

Summary

The Magento CMS provides you with the capability to customize your store without directly altering the XML and HTML files of your theme. You can build productive pages, static blocks, and widgets, adding increased functionality and buyer conveniences.

That being said, we should never shy away from rolling up our sleeves and diving into the actual theme files. By combining both disciplines, you have greatly elevated Magento's potential to meet your retailing needs.

In this chapter, we:

- Learned about Magento's CMS functionality
- Saw how to create and customize pages
- Explored the creation of static blocks
- Reviewed the many widgets available for your use

Now that our Store has products and content, it's time to let the world know that your store exists as a premiere online shopping destination.

7
Marketing Tools

The online marketplace is crowded. Thousands of new stores are going online each day. With Magento, you have one of the most powerful open source platforms for presenting and selling your products and services. But to be noticed—and to create valuable repeat business—you have to do more than just point a domain name to your store.

The key is marketing—presenting a selling proposition to potential customers that will entice them to at least visit your online showroom.

In this chapter, we will explore some of Magento's key marketing tools, including:

- Customer groups
- Promotions
- Newsletters
- Sitemaps
- Search engine optimization

As you prepare your store for launch, you need to spend some time becoming familiar with how these tools can help you attract and close more sales.

Customer groups

If you're new to e-commerce, you may not quite have a handle on how to group your potential customers, outside of retail and wholesale. Most of you will build retail stores, fewer will build wholesale businesses, and even fewer will do both.

Yet, if you give some careful thought to how you intend to market to your customers, you may find that there are more customer segments you need to identify. Here are examples of some other possible customer groups:

- Distributors who will re-sell your product to retailers
- Tax-exempt organizations, such as charities or government agencies
- Groups or teams, such as associations or athletic leagues
- Professionals, as opposed to hobbyists or amateurs
- Certified or approved buyers meeting a licensing or other qualification

Customer groups in Magento are not to be confused with customer profiles, such as age, sex, or preferences. A customer can only belong to one Magento group, so profile attributes cannot really be accommodated.

As you contemplate your **groups**, consider the following:

- Groups should be segments of your customer base that might have different pricing, benefits, or product focus
- Groups can be used (as we'll see later in this chapter) for specific marketing promotions using newsletters and promotional codes
- Groups can be assigned different tax classes for the purpose of charging (or not charging) sales tax

By default, Magento creates three Customer groups: General, Retailer, and Wholesale. When a customer registers in your store, they are automatically put into the General group. You can manually assign a customer to another group, either after they have registered or if you create the customer yourself in the administrative backend to your store.

Strangely enough, the Sample Data installation only creates one **Customer Tax Class**. Therefore, all the default Customer groups are assigned to the **Retail Customer Tax Class**. If you use other groups, you may want to create additional Customer Tax Classes (under **Sales | Tax | Customer Tax Classes**).

Creating a Customer group

Creating a new Customer group is perhaps the simplest operation in Magento!

1. Go to **Customers | Customer Groups** in your administration menu.

2. Click on **Add New Customer Group**.

3. Enter a **Group Name**.

4. Assign a **Tax Class** as created in *Chapter 5, Configuring to Sell*.

5. Click on **Save Customer Group**.

And that's all there is to it. Now that you understand how Customer groups are created in Magento, let's see how we can use these for marketing.

Promotions

Every retailer, with whom we work, finds it beneficial to offer promotions from time to time. From free shipping to coupons, promotions can help consumers choose your products over competitors, particularly if they feel they're getting a great bargain in the process.

As with Sales Tax, promotions are rule-based, meaning that the application and calculation of a promotion is based on rules you create. In Magento, there are two types of **Promotion Rules**:

1. **Catalog Price Rules** apply to any product that meets certain criteria. The discount is applied automatically.

2. **Shopping Cart Rules**, on the other hand, can be set to be only applied when a valid coupon is entered by the customer during Checkout. Shopping Cart Rules can also be applied automatically. Furthermore, Shopping Cart Rules— or **Coupons**—can be publicized by adding them to an RSS feed for your site.

Creating a Catalog Price Rule

As described, a Catalog Price Rule is a discount that is applied to selected products automatically. For example, using the installed Sample Data, let's assume you wish to provide a 5 percent discount on all Dell® brand products priced over 500 dollars sold between November 25, 2011 through November 27, 2011, as a Black Friday special.

Black Friday and Cyber Monday

For years, in the United States, the day after Thanksgiving—the last Friday of November, Black Friday—has been one of the busiest shopping days of the Christmas season. Retailers offer huge discounts and shoppers begin lining up well before dawn just to be the first one in the door. To counter the brick and mortar retailers, online retailers created Cyber Monday, the Monday following Black Friday, likewise offering huge discounts and special offers. Personally, I like the sound of Cyber Monday over the morbid moniker of Black Friday. I also like e-commerce!

Let's begin creating a new Catalog Price Rule:

1. Go to **Promotions | Catalog Price Rules**.
2. Click **Add New Rule**.
3. Enter the following in the **General Information** screen:

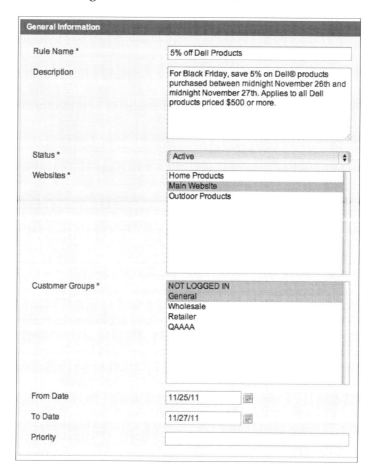

4. Click on **Conditions** in the left tab menu. Now, here's where it gets interesting!

5. Click the green plus sign to add a condition to your rule.

 Any underlined items in these screens can be clicked to reveal additional choices. Don't hesitate to click and discover!

6. In the drop-down menu that appears, choose **Brand**.

7. Click the ellipsis (**...**).

8. In the drop-down menu, choose **Dell**.

9. Click on the green plus sign again, and choose **Price** from the drop-down menu.

10. Click on **is**. Select **greater than** from the drop-down menu.

11. Click the following ellipsis. Enter **500.00** in the field and click outside the field.

Your conditions screen should look as follows:

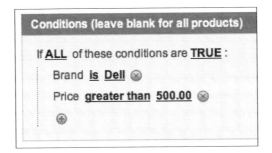

This promotion will now only apply to Dell brand products priced 500 dollars or more.

 The amount of the discount is based on the default currency for the website. If your site's default currency is Euros, then the discount would be 500 Euros.

Now, we need to create the discount calculation:

1. Click the **Actions** menu tab.

 The four choices for **Apply** give you tremendous flexibility, but may not be clearly understood.

2. **By Percentage of the Original Price** reduces the price of the product by the percentage specified, such as 15 percent off the price.

3. **By Fixed Amount** will reduce the product's price by a specified amount, such as 50 dollars off.

4. **To Percentage of the Original Price**, by contrast to **By Percentage of the Original Price**, sets the price at the percentage you enter. For example, if you enter 75, the price of the product would be 75 percent of its original price.

5. Likewise, **To Fixed Amount**, sets the price of the product at the price you enter instead of reducing the price by a fixed amount.

6. Since we're going to apply a percentage discount to the price of the product, we can leave **Apply** as is.

7. In **Discount Amount**, enter **5**.

8. If you do not want to apply any other Promotion Rules to these applicable products, choose **Yes** for **Stop Further Rules Processing**. For example, you may not want a customer to receive multiple discounts on the same product.

9. Click on **Save Rule**.

You now have a new rule that will automatically take effect at 12:01 AM on Friday, November 25 and run until 11:59 PM on Sunday, November 27. However, there is one final action to take!

Before your new rule can take effect, click **Apply Rules** at the top of the **Catalog Price Rules** page. Magento needs to set itself to apply the rules to the applicable products.

 For Catalog Price Rules to be effective, the Magento cron script must be running. I discuss triggering cron jobs in *Chapter 10, Advanced Techniques*.

Creating a Shopping Cart Rule

As a capitalizing entrepreneur, you've decided that while you're offering 5 percent off on Dell products for Black Friday, you want to give loyal customers a special coupon they can use on Cyber Monday only that will give them 15 percent off all orders of 250 dollars or more. What a generous retailer you are!

1. Go to **Promotions | Shopping Cart Price Rules**.

2. Click **Add New Rule**.

3. Enter the following in the **General Information** screen:

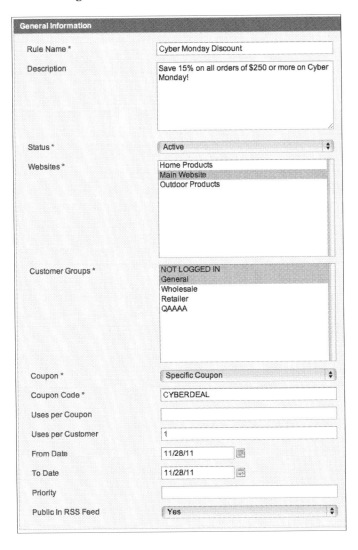

Let's talk a bit about some of the items on this screen, as there are differences between this and the one you completed for the previous Catalog Price Rule:

- You can use anything for the **Coupon Code**. However, you should use something that is easy to enter, yet unique enough not to be guessed (unless you don't mind that).

- If you want to restrict the number of times a coupon can be used, enter a value for **Uses per Coupon**. For instance, if you're only offering the discount to the first 100 people who use the coupon, enter **100**. Otherwise, leave blank if there is no limit.

- In many cases, you may want to limit the number of times a customer may use a coupon. In our example, we have limited the coupon use to once per customer by entering **1** for **Uses per Customer**.

Let's now create our conditions:

1. Click the **Conditions** menu tab.
2. Click the green plus sign. Choose **Subtotal**.
3. Click the ellipsis and enter **250.00**. Click outside the field.

Your condition should look as follows:

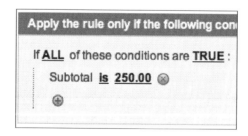

Next, we will create the discount action:

1. Click the **Actions** menu tab.
2. Select **Percent of product price discount** for **Apply**.

As with the Catalog Price Rules, the application methods for Shopping Cart Rules give you increased flexibility:

1. **Percent of product price discount** reduces the product price by the specified amount as a percentage of the product's price.
2. **Fixed amount discount** subtracts the amount from the product price, such as 10 dollars off.
3. **Fixed amount discount** for whole cart applies a fixed discount to the entire cart, not just selected products.
4. **Buy X get Y free (discount amount is Y)** really gives you a cool feature, allowing you to provide customers with a free product with the purchase of a qualifying product.

3. Enter **15** for the **Discount Amount**.

4. Select **Yes** for **Stop Further Rules Processing** if you want this to be the only discount applied to the shopping cart.

You'll also notice that on this screen you can also apply further rules specific to the products in the Shopping Cart. For instance, if you wanted this rule to only apply to Apple products, you could select Apple as a brand.

Also different from Catalog Price Rules, you can create a specific **Rule Label** for all Store Views, which you can also modify for specific Store Views. Click the **Labels** menu tab to enter what you want to appear to the customer after they enter their Coupon Code in their Shopping Cart.

On the **General Information** screen, at the bottom, is the choice to publicize your discounts in your site's RSS feed. Unless you really don't want people to know of a special discount, using your RSS feed will help push your discounts out to search engines and customers who may be subscribing to your RSS feed. This is an easy way to increase awareness, and search sites love RSS feeds.

Click **Save Rule** when you're finished setting up your rule. Unlike Catalog Price Rules, you do not have to apply the rules in order to have them activated.

Newsletters

One way to keep customers reminded about your store is to ask them to subscribe to receive periodic e-mail newsletters from you. By informing your customers about new products, special discounts, and more, you can many times generate repeat sales, which is the least expensive cost-per-sale you can have.

Reduce your cost-per-sale

Unless you have an established brand, you will need to advertise to attract buyers to your store. From pay-per-click online ads (for example, Google AdWords) to offline print ads, there are many ways of buying customer attention. However, you should always do whatever you can to encourage buyers to return again and again to buy from your store. You should also encourage referrals. These sales don't cost you any more in terms of advertising expenses. This is one reason social networks such as Facebook and Twitter have become so popular; they're free (actually, you can purchase advertising on both now). The idea is that by getting Facebook and Twitter users to mention their purchases, their friends may be inclined to shop with you. Again, this is free advertising and a zero cost-per-sale.

Effective use of newsletters, however, requires a certain degree of specialized knowledge and expertise—more than you may have if you're new to e-commerce, and certainly more than we can distill within this book. With social networking, we're seeing some shifts in newsletters, as well. More customers are opting out of newsletters, instead subscribing to Twitter feeds and Facebook pages to receive promotional information. Newsletters that contain more in-depth information and articles remain quite active, though.

That said, you should not hesitate to use newsletters, even if they are only minimally requested by your customers. The cost of production is minimal and there is no cost of delivery. Any sales they generate will certainly be worth the effort!

Designing a newsletter template

The most challenging aspect of setting up to send newsletters is creating your newsletter template. Personally, I would suggest you consider buying a template design you find suitable for your brand (we like Theme Forest (`http://www. themeforest.net`) for design templates), or hiring a designer with specific newsletter experience. If you do want to take a stab at designing your own newsletter template, here's some key advice:

- Keep the width of your newsletter to no more than 600 pixels, as many e-mail programs have narrow viewing windows.

- While you can put some CSS styles in the header to control overall styles, any specific styles for things such as paragraphs, spans, and so on should be in-line. That is, within the HTML tag itself.

- E-mail programs have trouble interpreting `<div>` tags properly. Unlike building contemporary web pages, use tables to lay out your design.

Back to 1999

If you're a web designer, you may be cringing over these guidelines for e-mail layouts. I do, as well. However, e-mail client programs don't all have the rendering capabilities of today's browsers. The variety of tools people use to read e-mail also contributes to this dilemma. As a designer, you're already faced with browser compatibility among four or five primary browsers and versions. Imagine trying to debug a complex layout for hundreds of different e-mail viewing possibilities?

I know it's not as fun as using stylesheets and `<div>` tags. Just consider it your opportunity to go down memory lane.

The use of templates for newsletters is a bit of a misnomer. The templates you create are not really used as you might imagine. You create a newsletter template in Magento to use for a particular e-mail event. If you wish to re-use the template for another mailing, but with some different content, you can save the original template as a new template.

Be that as it may, let's create a simple first newsletter template. Once you learn the basics of creating a Magento newsletter, you'll be prepared to apply more advanced design techniques or third-party newsletter design templates.

Let's put together a newsletter to send to customers announcing our Cyber Monday sale:

1. Go to **Newsletters | Newsletter Templates** in your administration backend.

2. Click on **Add New Template**.

3. For **Template Name**, enter **Cyber Monday**.

4. The **Template Subject** is what will appear as the subject of the e-mail your customers will receive. For this example, enter **Cyber Monday Sales Event!**

5. We'll leave **Sender Name** as is for now.

6. Enter your return e-mail address for the **Sender Email**. For our customers, we would enter **support@novusweb.com**.

7. In **Template Content**, I first add a couple of lines above the default content. What you see in this field, when you first create a new template, is so you'll know what Magento code to use to add an **Unsubscribe** link. This link allows recipients to unsubscribe from your newsletter list, and helps you meet anti-spam rules.

> Every country—and even some states in the US—have different anti-spam rules. If you're not familiar with the ones in your locale, do some research. That said, the main thing is to avoid having your server blacklisted or blocked by various **internet service providers (ISPs)**. The best way to avoid blacklisting is to prevent complaints by recipients: only send to customers who have agreed to receive your newsletter, have a clear and easy to find unsubscribe link, and include your company name and address. A link to your privacy policy page would also be advised.

8. Next, I create a table 600 pixels wide, one column in width, that has three rows. This way, I can include a header, a main content area, and a footer. If I need to further subdivide any of these areas, I can always nest a table within a table cell. By clicking the **Inserts New Table** icon in the editor tool bar, a pop-up window, shown in the following screenshot, allows me to specify the table I want to insert:

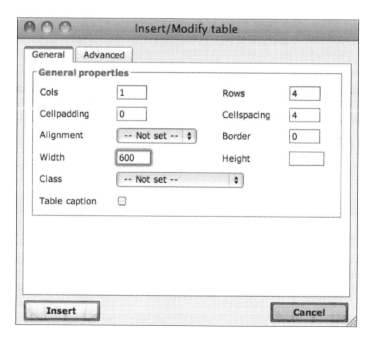

In the following screenshot, you can see the very simple newsletter design I created for this example. By using the tools in the editor, I styled the different table cells.

Additionally, as you can see in the bottom pane, I added some CSS styling that will be placed in the header of the e-mail. Remember, we want to use as little styling in the header as necessary.

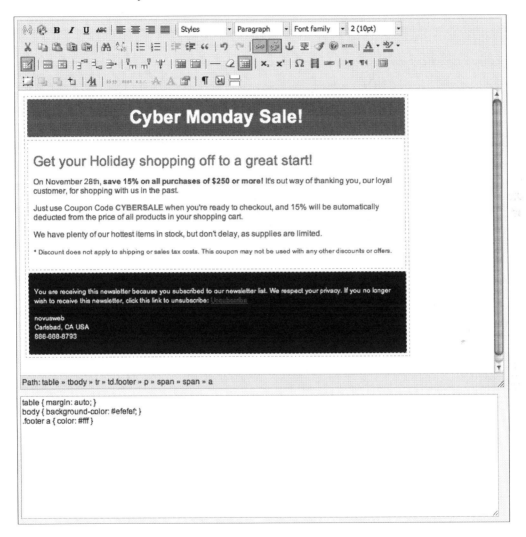

Notice the blue link in the footer area. While I have added a CSS statement—**.footer a { color: #fff; }**—in the Template Styles pane, Magento won't render these styles until we preview the template.

To do that, click **Save Template** at the top of the screen. You'll be returned to the list of newsletter templates. To the right of your template, choose **Preview** in the **Action** drop-down menu. A new browser window will open, and you can see the fruits of your labor. In my case, the preview looks as follows:

Cyber Monday Sale!

Get your Holiday shopping off to a great start!

On November 28th, **save 15% on all purchases of $250 or more!** It's out way of thanking you, our loyal customer, for shopping with us in the past.

Just use Coupon Code CYBERSALE when you're ready to checkout, and 15% will be automatically deducted from the price of all products in your shopping cart.

We have plenty of our hottest items in stock, but don't delay, as supplies are limited.

* Discount does not apply to shipping or sales tax costs. This coupon may not be used with any other discounts or offers.

You are receiving this newsletter because you subscribed to our newsletter list. We respect your privacy. If you no longer wish to receive this newsletter, click this link to unsubscribe: Unsubscribe

novusweb
Carlsbad, CA USA
866-668-8793

This looks pretty much as we expected.

You can also insert Static Blocks (see *Chapter 6, Managing Non-product Content*) into the body of your newsletter using the following format: **{{block type="cms/block" block_id="block-id"}}**.

One more thing. To create the **Unsubscribe** link as shown in the footer, simply create a text link as you normally would using the built-in editor. For the link URL, enter **{{var subscriber.getUnsubscriptionLink()}}**. This will dynamically create a link your subscribers can click on to go to a special page on your site to unsubscribe.

Sending a newsletter

Once you have your template designed—and customers who have subscribed, of course—you can queue your newsletter to send. From the list of newsletter templates, select **Queue newsletter...** in the **Action** drop-down menu.

From this **Edit Newsletter** screen, you can set the start date for your newsletter, choose subscribers from any or all of your Stores, and make any last minute changes to the newsletter template. Once you've finished on this screen, click **Save Newsletter** to set your e-mail in motion.

After saving, you will be taken to the **Newsletter Queue** screen where you can view the status of your newsletter, including the start and finish time, the current status, how many e-mails have been processed, and how recipients are scheduled to receive your newsletter.

 Magento generally sends newsletter e-mails in batches—usually 15 at a time—so don't be surprised to see the number of processed e-mails increment in stages, rather than all at once.

Sitemaps

In the world of web development, there are two ways sitemaps are used:

- As a Table of Contents, of sorts, as a page on the site listing all publicly available pages
- An XML file stored on the server and used by search engines

The content of both is quite similar: the pages of your site. Yet, each are constructed a bit differently, since the first type is part of your public website and the latter is only seen by search engines.

The Magento sitemap

Magento automatically creates a public sitemap page for your site. However, unlike sitemaps created in platforms such as WordPress, the Magento sitemap merely lists the categories and products within your product catalog. In fact, there is little to configure (or possible to configure) with the Magento sitemap page.

To enable the sitemap page, follow these steps:

1. Go to **System | Configuration | Catalog**.
2. Expand the **Search Engine Optimizations** panel.
3. Select **Enable** for **Autogenerated Search Terms**.
4. Click on **Save Config**.

(We'll be addressing many of the other items in this panel in the later section on Search Engine Optimization.)

The configuration settings for the sitemap page are under **System | Configuration | Catalog**, in the **Sitemap** panel, as shown here:

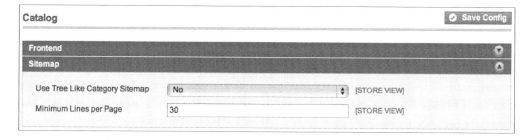

As you can see, you can only configure whether you want category lists in a tree-like hierarchy, and what the minimum number of items you want listed on a single web page is.

There are several third-party extensions available for Magento that add additional layout functionality to the built-in sitemap page. See **Magento Connect** for the latest modules (http://www.magentocommerce.com/magento-connect/filter/all?query=sitemap).

The Google Sitemap

While Magento refers to the XML sitemap as the Google Sitemap, it really is a standard-format XML file that can be used by Yahoo!, Bing, and other search engines. These sites use the sitemap to understand more about the content of your site. While search engines regularly crawl websites by following the links on pages, the XML sitemap gives them direct links to all the content on your site.

Configuring the XML sitemap for your site takes several steps:

1. Configure the Google Sitemap settings.
2. Generate the sitemap files.
3. Submit the sitemap URL to the search engines.

Configuring the Google Sitemap

Under **System | Configuration | Google Sitemap** in your Magento backend are four panels visible if your **Current Configuration Scope** is **Default Config**. Each of the top three allow you to set how often the information on your site is updated, and its relative priority on a scale of 0 to 1.

For example, the default settings provide for a priority of 0.5, 1, and 0.25 for **Categories**, **Products**, and **CMS Pages**, respectively. If you are an e-commerce store, changes to your products should receive the highest priority; categories are secondary; and, lastly, the other content of your site—the CMS pages—are of the lowest priority.

> Unless you have specific needs for altering these default values, I would suggest you leave them as they are.

The fourth panel—only visible at the **Default Config** scope level— is called **Generation Settings**. Magento has the ability to automatically generate new sitemap files periodically according to the settings within this panel. However, configuring this panel alone does not actually mean your XML sitemap files will be automatically generated.

In *Chapter 10, Advanced Techniques*, you'll learn how to trigger cron jobs in Magento to periodically perform certain functions, including generating sitemaps.

So what if you can't configure a **crontab**? Is all lost? No. At least not as far as sitemaps are concerned. As we'll see in the next section, you can manually generate your XML sitemaps as often as you please. In fact, if you rarely update your site, say about every week or so, you really don't need to worry about automatically creating your sitemaps. Simply add the manual generation step to your updating activities.

Ask for help

As with any complex application, we sometimes find, from time to time, certain inadequacies with Magento that are at times frustrating. Sometimes they're even showstoppers. The management of scheduled tasks in Magento is certainly not a showstopper, but it is a bit frustrating.

When I started out with Magento, I assumed, as many do, that by configuring the **Generation Settings** in the backend, my sitemaps would be automatically generated. As we know now, that is not the case.

You'll periodically come across issues with Magento like this one that seem to be real head-scratchers. Books like this one are created to help resolve these questions. However, when it comes to crontabs, unless you're a real Unix hack—and especially if you're not hosting your Magento store on a Linux/Unix server—defer to the real techies that understand this issue: your hosting provider.

Like the man who refuses to stop and ask directions when driving, I hardly ever turn to my hosting provider unless the issue is behind what I'm focusing on: building, configuring, and delivering a quality Magento store for my client. Getting under the hood with Unix is one of those times.

If I can at least flag those areas which are outside the expertise of most of my readers, then I can help turn what might be a showstopper into a successful implementation.

Generating the sitemap files

Now that you have your configuration settings, the next step is to create the actual XML sitemap file:

1. Go to **Catalog | Google Sitemap** in your backend.
2. Click on **Add Sitemap**.
3. Enter a **Name** for your sitemap file. While it is assumed, from this screen, that any name can be used, in fact, only `sitemap.xml` is acceptable to Magento.

4. If you wish to store the sitemap files within a directory on your server, you can specify the **Path**. The directory must have write permissions.

5. Finally, choose the **Store View** for which the sitemap file applies.

6. Click on **Save and Generate**.

Generating sitemaps for multiple stores

Since Magento will only allow `sitemap.xml` as a filename, how can you generate multiple sitemap files for each **Store View**?

The answer is to create subdirectories for each store's `sitemap.xml` file. For example, if we want to create a sitemap for our Outdoor English-language store, we might create a subdirectory within our Magento installation called `sitemaps-outdoor`. By specifying this **Path** in our sitemap configuration, our sitemap file will be stored in that directory.

The following screenshot shows how I configured a sitemap for our Outdoor English language store:

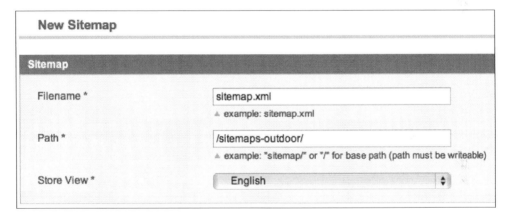

Once you have the sitemap generated, you can manually generate the sitemap as needed by clicking on **Generate** on the row of the intended sitemap.

Submitting your sitemap

When you register your website with **Google Webmaster Tools** or **Bing/Yahoo! Webmaster Tools**, you will be asked to provide a sitemap for your site. Once your sitemap is generated, the Google Sitemap screen will show you the full path to your sitemap in the link for Google column.

Simply copy this full URL path and use it whenever a search engine asks for a sitemap file.

You can see what the search engines see by pasting this URL into your browser location bar. Depending on your browser, you may see the actual XML code or an interpretation of the code as an RSS feed.

Search engine optimization

The subject of **search engine optimization** can be, as you probably know, a very lengthy discussion worthy of several books. For our intentions, we want to go over some of the tools that are inherent in Magento to assist you with the process of adding search engine friendly attributes to your online store.

Magento wisely includes convenient fields so you can manage the meta keywords, meta description, page title, and URLs for the categories, products and CMS pages in your site. If you invest the time to manage these attributes, you'll find your site will be much better catalogued by the search engines.

Global SEO settings

The first place to start is to define the default settings for your page attributes at the website and store levels. If you don't individually enter values for these fields at the category, product, or CMS level, you still want some value to be included.

While global settings are convenient, you should take the time to configure the individual page attributes whenever possible, as duplicate content across your site — multiple pages with the same SEO attributes — can work against you.

URLs

By default, a Magento URL looks like this:

```
http://www.sitedomain.com/index.php/furniture/living-room/ottoman.
html
```

While this certainly works, it's better to shorten this URL when possible. By using the **URL Rewrites** configuration in Magento, our URL will now look like this:

```
http://www.sitedomain.com/furniture/living-room/ottoman.html
```

1. Go to **System | Configuration | Web**.
2. Expand the **Search Engines Optimization** panel.
3. Select **Yes** for **Use Web Server Rewrites**.
4. Click on **Save Config**.

Now, let's go one step further. Let's remove the .html from the end of our URLs. This will even further shorten our URL and leave it nice and clean.

1. Go to **System | Configuration | Catalog**.
2. Expand the **Search Engine Optimizations** panel.
3. Remove .html from both **Product URL Suffix** and **Category URL Suffix**, leaving both fields blank.
4. In most cases, we do want to set **Use Categories Path for Product URLs** to **Yes**, as this automatically adds the category name to the URL, which could be good for search engine searches. However, if you have several layers of categories, or if your URLs will be more than 255 characters, consider setting this to **No**.
5. You should also select **Yes** for both **Use Canonical Link Meta Tag for Categories** and **Use Canonical Link Meta Tag for Products**. This adds a meta tag in your page header that helps prevent search engines from penalizing you for any pages that may have duplicate content on them.
6. Click on **Save Config**.
7. Go to **System | Cache Management** and flush your Magento cache.

The following is an example of what the **Search Engine Optimizations** panel should look like:

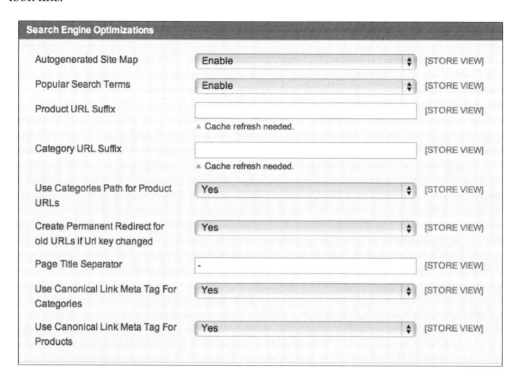

Default meta tags

To configure your default meta tags:

1. Go to **System | Configuration | Web**.

2. Expand the **HTML Head** panel.

3. If you have multiple websites or stores, and you want different default information for each, select the proper **Current Configuration Scope** in the upper-left part of your screen.

4. Enter a **Default Title** that will appear at the top of your visitors' browser window. This will be overridden by any specific choices made at the category or CMS page level. However, where these specific entries are not made, this title will appear. This is also the title that will appear on your home page.

5. The **Title Prefix** and **Title Suffix** fields allow you to automatically include words to appear before and after any specified page title. For example, if the page title for a product is *Sony VAIO Computer*, we could have Magento prepend *Buy* before the page title, and *at Bret's Electronics* after the title, thereby creating a page title of *Buy Sony VAIO Computer at Bret's Electronics*. Of course, the word *Buy* would appear even before a CMS page, such as *Buy About Us*. Therefore, experiment to find what words work best.

Personally, I only use the **Title Suffix**, leaving the specified page title without any prefix.

6. Enter a **Default Description**. Again, this will also serve as the meta description for your home page.

7. Likewise for **Default Keywords**.

Meta keywords

While including keywords won't penalize you, major search engines generally ignore the meta keywords tag. Years ago, webmasters would load up this tag with lots of keywords, including words that had nothing to do with the actual page content, but were intended to draw online visitors. Long ago, search engines caught on to this keyword spamming technique. I personally don't worry about the meta keyword field.

8. If you want the search engines to index all the pages in your site (and really, what e-commerce store doesn't?), leave **Default Robots** set for **INDEX, FOLLOW**.

9. Click on **Save Config**.

Based on these instructions, here's a sample **HTML Head** panel:

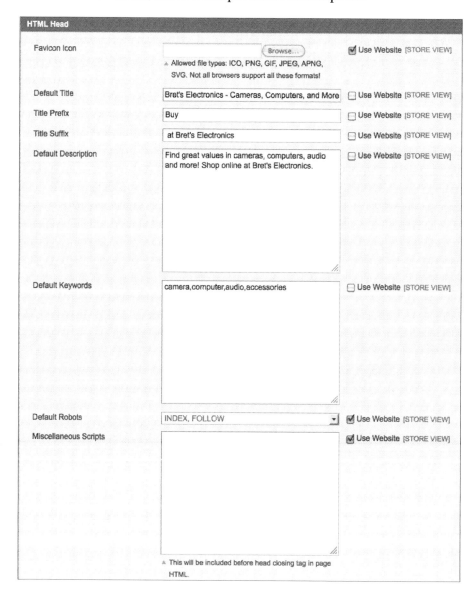

Setting page-level attributes

Whether you're editing a category, a product, or a CMS page, you have specific control over the page title, meta description, meta keywords, and URL for that item.

As an example, let's review the process for managing the SEO attributes for a product:

1. Under **Catalog | Manage Products**, click on a listed product.

2. In the **General** panel, look at the **URL key** field. By default, Magento takes the name of the product, converts all characters to lowercase, and replaces spaces with hyphens. This value is what becomes the last part of the URL for this product. For instance, `http://www.sitedomain.com/htc-touch-diamond` is the URL for one of the Sample Data products where the URL key is set to *htc-touch-diamond*.

> You may feel the need to add or edit the URL key field. If you do so, you'll see a checkbox labeled **Create Permanent Redirect for old URL**. By checking this box, Magento will create an automatic redirect from the original URL for this product to the new one you have entered once you save. This is convenient if your product has already been indexed by the search engines, as you don't want the old link appearing in a search results page if clicking on the link results in a **404 Not Found** error for the visitor. With a redirect, clicking on the old link will take the visitor to the new URL automatically.

3. Next, click **Meta Information** on the left tab menu.

4. By default, the meta fields on this page are blank. You can enter whatever values you wish to here, and Magento will replace any default values with your entries.

5. Click on **Save** when finished and clear the Magento cache to see your changes.

Automatic product meta values

Earlier, we discussed how to set default values for the page title, meta description, and meta keywords. Guess what? Magento takes automation even further!

If you do not enter any values for these meta tags for an individual product, Magento automatically generates these values as follows:

- For **page title**, Magento uses a combination of the product name and the category hierarchy, separated by hyphens. For example, for the HTC Touch Diamond product, the page title is *HTC Touch Diamond - Cell Phones - Electronics*. If we have configured a **Title Prefix** and **Title Suffix**, as we did earlier, these are appended to this default title, rendering something like *Buy HTC Touch Diamond - Cell Phones - Electronics at Bret's Electronics*.

- The **meta description** is generated using whatever you have entered as the **Short Description** for the product.

- **Meta keywords** are simply the product name. Unfortunately, no commas are inserted between the words, but, as noted before, meta keywords are no longer an important SEO consideration.

For categories, Magento will automatically create a page title, but it will use the default meta description and keywords you specify in the system configuration unless you specifically add values under **Catalog | Manage Categories**.

Summary

When I began building websites in 1995, all we had to do was launch the site to get noticed, as there wasn't much online competition back then. Today, it's a very competitive landscape.

While your store marketing plans will certainly include many disciplines, such as pay-per-click advertising, social networking, and more, Magento helps you in terms of promoting your site and making it more search-engine friendly.

Together, we covered:

- Managing customer groups
- Promotion and coupons
- Designing and sending e-mail newsletters
- Generating sitemaps for visitors and search engines
- Configuring meta information useful for search engine optimization

At this point, your site is pretty much ready to go! If you've gone through the process of installing and configuring your Magento site to this point, you're ready to start taking orders. How exciting!

I would like to add at this point that while we have conquered configurations for Magento, much of the work in creating a successful online store lies in your marketing efforts. Simply publishing products online will not create sales; you need to consistently utilize the built-in tools of Magento—RSS feeds, newsletters, promotions, and so on—to publicize and promote. If you're the one in charge of creating sales, learn how to use the many other tools of the Internet, such as blogs, product search sites, and more, to bring attention to your store and its products. The technical work may be done, but the process of bringing customers to your shop is just beginning.

As you begin working with your store—and particularly if you're in charge of the technical aspects of the installation—you'll want to take Magento even further, to add on to its capabilities. In the next chapter, we will cover how to extend Magento.

8
Extending Magento

One of Magento's strengths is the fact that the platform can be extended to provide additional features and functions. These extensions—or modules—number in the thousands. They include themes, payment gateway integrations, site management enhancements, utilities, and many, many more.

In this chapter, we will discuss the two primary ways of extending Magento:

- Installing third-party extensions through **Magento Connect**
- Creating your own Magento extensions

By learning how Magento can be enhanced, you will find that the power of Magento can be broadened to meet almost any specific e-commerce need you might imagine.

Magento Connect

Third-party extensions that are offered to the Magento community are, for the most part, listed in a special section of the Magento website called Magento Connect (http://www.magentocommerce.com/magento-connect/).

The Magento Connect site, as shown in the following screenshot, was completely revamped in October 2011 giving it a much more Web 2.0 experience:

Let's now review some of the features of Magento Connect as they relate to researching possible add-ons for your Magento installation.

Searching Magento Connect

At the center-right of the Magento Connect home page is a search field. As with any intuitive search, simply enter in one or more keywords. You can also select the specific version—which Magento calls *platform*—in the drop-down menu to the right of the keyword entry field. As shown in the following screenshot, we are searching for any extension relating to **google**:

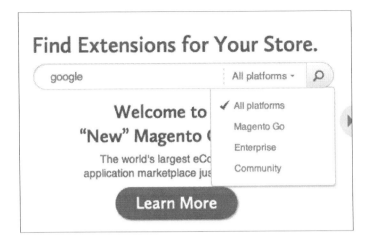

Furthermore, we can narrow our search to the specific Magento platform, such as the one on which this book is focused: **Community**.

The results of our search can be further refined by identifying extensions that are free versus paid, and, if paid, fall within a certain price range.

You can also browse the extensions using the categories in the top navigation bar, or the groupings listed below the search form on the main Magento Connect page.

Why developers create free extensions

Magento **extensions** take time to create, test, package, and distribute. Additionally, responsible developers provide support to those who install their extensions. Considering this investment of time and effort, why would any developer offer a free extension?

- In some cases, the free extension is a lite or less-featured version of a paid extension. If you like how the lite version works in your Magento installation, you might pay to get additional functionality.

- Some extension developers provide other paid extensions, as well. Again, if you like how the free extension works, you might be more trusting of the developer's paid extensions. This is particularly popular among theme developers who create one or more free themes with modest features, but sell much more feature-laden themes.

- I downloaded an extension once, that did exactly what it promised, but I needed it to do something slightly different. Rather than change the code myself, I hired the extension developer to create a modified version to meet my needs. I ended up paying a lot less than if I had hired a developer to create the entire extension from scratch.

- Finally, there are developers who simply like to share. Amazing as it may seem, some people actually like to contribute to the overall success of Magento. Of course, I'm being cheeky here, but in many cases a developer has created a solution for their own needs that they realize could benefit others in the world of Magento. By providing a free extension or theme, the developer is also validating their expertise. If I need to hire a developer for a specific Magento need, I would first look to developers who have solved similar issues. For example, if I need a payment gateway extension that doesn't already exist, I would first look to those developers who have demonstrated their ability to successfully create payment gateway integrations for Magento. A free extension, therefore, becomes a portfolio piece for a developer.

Trusted extensions

As you view various extensions, you'll no doubt see some that are marked as a trusted extension. These are add-ons which have been judged by Magento to meet certain requirements in terms of coding, security, and performance. At the time of this writing, Magento is only evaluating extensions for its **Magento Go** hosted solution, but the indication is that this process will extend to all Magento platforms, such as **Enterprise** and **Community**.

Evaluating extensions

In lieu of an official designation, such as a trusted extension, how should you go about determining which extensions and themes are best for your use? While the process of enhancing your Magento store is bound to be one of trial and error at one time or another, I have my own process of evaluation which you may find useful.

Is the extension popular?

If lots of other developers have downloaded the extension, that indicates that the extension is probably one that solves a need for a great many installations. As shown in the following screenshot, the **Magento EasyTabs** extension (http://www.magentocommerce.com/magento-connect/magento-easytabs.html) has been downloaded over 20,000 times.

This extension adds tabs to the product detail page for a number of content items, such as description, specifications, reviews, and more. It also provides tabs for CMS pages. This makes product detail pages more compact and better highlights important information for shoppers.

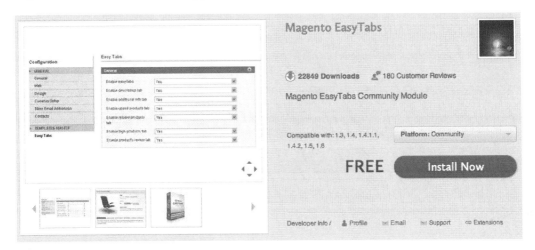

What do others think about the extension?

I look to see if there are a number of entries under the **User reviews** tab. Why many of these so-called reviews are actually support requests, where some developers post kudos or complaints about the extension. In other cases, developers point out the cases in which the extension does not work, or has a conflict with another extension.

Reading the reviews can help you get a sense of any difficulties or challenges you may have in using the extension.

Does the extension developer provide support?

There are several ways an extension developer can provide support. Even with free extensions, I try to gauge how responsive the developer will be to any problems I might encounter:

- Does the developer respond to issues in the **User reviews** section?
- Does the developer provide documentation for installation and use?
- Do their Release Notes clearly document the changes and impact of newer updates?

If posted user issues go unanswered for weeks, I usually avoid the extension. As with most developers, our projects cannot be held up indefinitely waiting for a developer to respond to a support question.

Is there a trial or lite version?

If the previous three evaluations do not satisfy me, but I still find the extension appealing, I might go ahead and install the extension to try it if I can install it without having to invest money. I have no problem paying for an obscure extension with no visible support as long as I know it will work. I might query the developer once I have installed the free version in order to get a sense of their support before buying the full license, though.

A precautionary tale

Even the most well-meaning extension is not necessarily perfect. Some extensions don't play well together. Others may be affected by any custom permissions. And still others can throw fatal errors making your store instantly inaccessible.

I learned a long time ago—and by trusting that a popular extension surely wouldn't hurt my store—to follow certain rules when adding new extensions to a Magento installation:

- First, I have created a test installation, much like the one I installed to write this book. It is installed into its own account at our hosting provider.

- Second, I install extensions and themes to test how well they work. Once they prove worthy, and if I feel they may be worthwhile for current and future Magento installations, I leave them on the test installation. As I add future add-ons, I will want to be sure that they continue to behave nicely with my existing, preferred extensions.

- Third, I keep an internal wiki on installing and configuring a new Magento installation. New extensions are added to this wiki, including notes on installation, extension keys and links to documentation. It's also wise to include version numbers and vendor names in your list.

By adhering to this methodology, I am able to keep our Magento installations solid and unaffected by extensions that misbehave.

Installing extensions

There is a distinct difference between installing free and paid extensions. Free extensions are installed using the built-in **Magento Connect Manager** in your Magento installation. Paid extensions require manual installation.

Using the Magento Connect Manager

If you want to install a free extension, you first need to be a registered user on the Magento website. Once you're registered:

1. Click on the **Install Now** button.

2. Select **Magento Connect 2.0** from the top drop-down menu. (1.0 is for earlier, older versions previous to 1.4.2.)

3. Select the checkbox labeled **I agree to the extension license agreement**.

4. Click on **Get Extension Key**.

A URL will appear where the **Get Extension Key** button was, as in the following screenshot:

This is the URL you will use with the Magento Connect Manager. Copy it to your clipboard.

1. Log into your Magento backend.

2. Go to **System | Magento Connect | Magento Connect Manager**.

3. Log into the **Magento Connect Manager** using your Magento administrative login credentials.

4. In the field labeled **Paste extension key to install**, paste in the extension key you copied from the Magento Connect website. (See the following screenshot.)

5. Click **Install**.

6. After the Magento Connect Manager validates the key, you can click **Proceed**.

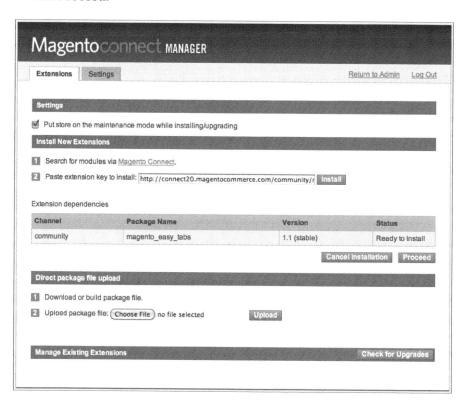

At the bottom of the page, an old-style terminal window will show the progress of the installation and let you know if it was successful, or if errors occurred. The following screenshot shows the successful installation of the EasyTabs extension:

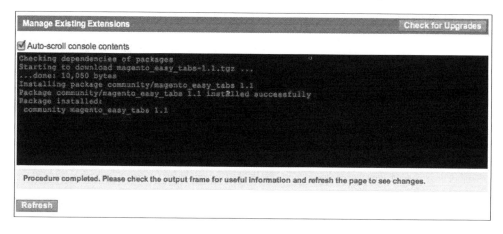

Once you have installed your new extension, you should:

1. Return to the Magento backend.

2. Empty all caches under **System | Cache Management**.

3. Log out and log back into the Magento backend.

4. Proceed with any configuration instructions provided by the extension developer.

Manually installing extensions

Most paid extensions, as well as some free extensions, are not installed using the Magento Connect Manager. Since paid extensions are sold at the developers' websites, there is no extension key to use with the Magento Connect Manager.

In *Chapter 4, Designs and Themes*, we discussed the installation of themes. In like fashion, non-theme extensions that must be manually installed are generally installed using FTP. Each extension will contain various folders and files that reside in various parts of your Magento installation. Additionally, manually installed extensions sometimes include additional instructions to modify certain files, either in your existing theme files or in the Magento core files.

Developer beware

If an extension for Magento 1.5 or above requires that you modify any core Magento files, be very careful. This is not the preferred coding practice as prescribed by Magento, as future updates to Magento could easily render your extension inoperable.

This is another reason I use a test installation, as described earlier. If installing a new extension caused a problem, you may find it difficult to diagnose.

As with free extensions, use diligence when buying extensions. Since paid extensions do not have a download count in their Magento Connect listing, you have no indication as to the popularity of a paid extension. Therefore, ask around. Browse the online Magento discussion boards. Try to find out what experience other developers have had with a particular extension or extension developer.

Building extensions

If you're a strong PHP developer, you may find it beneficial to create your own Magento enhancements. In fact, if you've been working with Magento for any length of time, you've no doubt had cause to tweak the code, perhaps, adding new functionality. For those with experience in MVC object-oriented programming, building new functionality for Magento can be quite rewarding.

Obviously, going into an in-depth programming discussion about PHP programming is not within the scope of this book. However, if you do plan to create an extension you would like to share with other Magento developers, whether for free or profit, you should know about certain guidelines and resources that can help you create an extension that will be well-received by the Magento community.

Whether others have gone before

If you can't find an extension for Magento to meet your needs and you think you want to do your own enhancements, take a moment to do some online searching first. One of the first places I look is the Magento Wiki (`http://www.magentocommerce.com/wiki`). At the time of this writing, the Magento Wiki is a bit disheveled and in need of a thorough cleaning, but within its pages are some nifty nuggets.

For example, one contributor added a considerable entry on how to add a security question for customers who forgot their password (`http://www.magentocommerce.com/wiki/5_-_modules_and_development/customers_and_accounts/forgot_password_security_qa`). This is not an inherent functionality in Magento, yet it can be added by following the instructions in this wiki entry. By tapping into these contributed tutorials and examples, you will learn a lot about how Magento is structured and how you can enhance its underpinnings.

You can also search on Google for possible solutions for your issue. There are numerous blogs where developers freely share some significant solutions. One of my favorites is the **Inchoo blog** (`http://inchoo.net/blog/`). Another good one is hosted by **Yireo** (`http://www.yireo.com`). These Magento experts have tackled some very interesting challenges with some quite elegant solutions. I also post solutions and tweaks on our website (`http://www.novusweb.com`).

Therefore, before you dive into your own modifications, check around. Why start from scratch if others have already done most of the work for you?

Creating an extension package

Magento extensions (including themes) that are to be distributed via Magento Connect must be packaged. That is, they must contain certain elements in order for users to use the Magento Connect Manager. For paid extensions, using the Magento packaging process insures that your extension, even though manually installed, is properly configured in terms of required files and components for operation within Magento. In fact, Magento requires that you use the Magento Connect Manager to package any extension for Magento.

For our purposes here, we will go over the process of creating a free Magento extension. Paid extensions use much the same process, except that you don't upload the package to Magento Connect; you distribute it through your own website once the customer has paid you.

We are also going to focus on what are called **2.0 extensions**. While you can provide backward-compatibility to older versions, our concentration continues to be on Magento Community version 1.5 and above.

Before beginning the process of packaging your extension, go to the Magento Connect website and register (just as you did in order to obtain an extension key in the earlier section of this chapter).

Your extension files

For your new extension to work, it must be placed correctly within the Magento file hierarchy:

- Functional code for an extension should be placed in the `app/code/community` or `app/code/local` directories, depending on your preference.

- Your extension can have its own hierarchy. For example, **Brets_SEOTool** could reside in `app/code/community/Brets/SEOTool`, with `SEOTool` containing the various `Block`, `controllers`, `Helper`, `Model`, and `sql` folders and files.

- Layout updates to the administrative UI are contained in `app/design/adminhtml/default/default/layout/brets_seotool.xml` (to continue our example).

- Administrative template files are placed in `app/design/adminhtml/default/default/template/brets_seotool/`.

- If you have layout updates for the public store view, these updates are managed by `app/design/frontend/base/default/layout/brets_seotool.xml`.

- Likewise, template updates are put into `app/design/frontend/base/default/template/brets_seotool.xml`.

- At a minimum, you should provide a U.S. localization translation file as `app/locale/en_US/Brets_SEOTool.csv`. You can also provide other translation files, if you wish.

- Finally, the needed file that tells Magento to activate your extension (and allows the administrator to enable or disable it) is `app/etc/modules/Brets_SEOTool.xml`.

Pay attention to the capitalization shown in this and ongoing examples.

Creating your package information

If your enhancement is installed in your Magento installation and you're ready to package it:

1. Log into your Magento backend.
2. Go to **System | Magento Connect | Package Extensions**.

The package process entails five distinct steps: **Package Info**, **Release Info**, **Authors**, **Dependencies**, and **Contents**. Let's begin with the first step:

1. Enter the **Name** of your extension. Use only letters and substitute any spaces with underscores, so that *Bret's SEOTool* becomes *Brets_SEOTool*. This name must also match the name of your add-on, including capitalization.
2. For **Channel**, enter community if you are using Magento version 1.5 or later. Enter *magento-community* if your current installation is 1.4 or older.
3. Likewise, select the compatibility of your extension by selecting either 1.5.0.0 and later or Pre-1.5.0.0 for Support releases.
4. Enter descriptions of your extension in both the **Summary** and **Description** fields. Do not include links in these fields.
5. Enter the name of the software license under which you wish to release your extension. While you can create any license you like for a paid extension, you must use one of the open source licenses for any free extension. For a good list and explanation of open source licenses, see `http://www.opensource.org/licenses`.

 Before releasing your extension, you should be aware of the different types of open source licenses available. There are subtle differences between them. If you choose to release a paid extension, you do have to make sure that your commercial software license doesn't conflict with the license used by Magento for its community version.

If you are using an open source license, you may enter the URL of the license in the **License URL** field.

Release information

You can use any type of numbering you wish to denote release version. However, you must increment it with each subsequent upload if you change any files within your package.

Release Stability refers to how you want users to consider your extension. Is it ready for prime time? Or should those who install your extension be more cautious? You can choose any level you wish. The one caveat: if you choose **Development**, Magento will not allow your package to be installed by others. You can upload it, but until you deem your extension to be at **Alpha** or above, it cannot be installed.

The **Notes** field is required. You should enter any particular information you feel is important for the particular release, such as *This is a Beta version. Do not install on a production server until you have fully tested it.*

Authors

Of course, you should enter your own information. By authors, Magento is referring to registered users that are responsible for maintaining the package. Use your Magento Connect account username (not your screen name) for the **User** field.

Dependencies

While it may be difficult to test your extension for a wide variety of PHP versions, if you're a strong PHP coder, you probably know which versions are applicable. If not, you may need to restrict your versions to the ones in which you are most confident. These would primarily be the versions under which your current version of Magento Community is compatible. Your package may require other Magento packages or certain PHP extensions.

Contents

Here's where we get to the nitty-gritty of your package. On this screen, you add all the files of your package.

Target is the part of the Magento architecture into which the file or directory is to be placed. The following are the paths of these various choices:

- **Magento Local module file**: `/app/code/local`
- **Magento Community module file**: `/app/code/community`

- **Magento Core team module file**: /app/code/core
- **Magento User Interface (layouts, templates)**: /app/design
- **Magento Global Configuration**: /app/etc
- **Magento PHP Library file**: /lib
- **Magento Locale language file**: /app/locale
- **Magento Media library**: /media
- **Magento Theme Skin (Images, CSS, JS)**: /skin
- **Magento Other web accessible file**: /
- **Magento PHPUnit test**: /tests
- **Magento other**: /

In the **Path** field you enter the path of your directory or file relative to the paths listed previously. If your language file is located at app/locale/en_US/Brets_SEOTool. csv, you would enter /en_US/Brets_SEOTool.csv.

Select the **Type** of content, whether it is a file or a **recursive directory**. A recursive directory means that all folders and files within that directory will be included in your package.

If you want to include or exclude certain files or folders within a recursive directory, you can enter regular expressions into the fields **Include** and/or **Ignore**.

Pull the trigger

Once you have completed all the various screens, you can save and create your package by clicking on **Save Data and Create Package**. Magento will then gather all the indicated content folders and files, create a package data XML file, and compress it all into a .tgz file. You're now ready to distribute your new extension.

Need I say it?

Of course, despite your most careful intentions, your first try at creating a package may not produce a perfect outcome. To be sure, you should first manually install your package into another Magento installation that meets your extension's minimum requirements. Don't rush to push out an untested and untried product. The Magento community will certainly let you know about it!

Upload your extension

Your finished extension can now be uploaded into Magento Connect. Even if you're distributing a paid extension, you do want to list it in Magento Connect, where thousands go each day to search for ways to enhance their Magento store.

The uploading process is quite simple and straightforward. To begin, log into the Magento website and go to **My Account**. Click on **Add New Extension** and follow the instructions shown.

 At the time of writing, the Magento Connect site was still evolving. However, the extension uploading process still appears to be an easy process. For the latest information on submitting extensions, go to http://www.magentocommerce.com/magento-connect/create_your_extension/.

Summary

Almost every week, I search Magento Connect just to see what new features and themes are being added. The creativity of the Magento developer community can be quite impressive.

One of the greatest joys of working with Magento is knowing that it is fully extendable in many ways, from simple theme enhancements to full-fledged functionality changes. Depending on your own skills and talents, you may want to take solutions you've created and let others benefit, either as free contributions or money-making add-ons.

In this chapter, we covered:

- Searching, evaluating, and installing Magento Connect extensions
- The process of packaging your own extensions

Of course, we have a couple more interesting areas to cover in *Chapter 9, Optimizing Magento*, and *Chapter 10, Advanced Techniques*, which will further help you extend the power of Magento.

9
Optimizing Magento

As you've no doubt realized by now that Magento is a very powerful e-commerce platform. From its robust product management suite to its virtually unlimited extendability, Magento packs a lot into one open source platform.

From our work within its files, we have learned that Magento combines a great number of separate files and data tables to present any page to online visitors. By its very nature, the MVC architecture of Magento puts a good deal of overhead on any web server. In the beginning, the complexity of Magento discouraged some developers because of the demands the platform placed on hosting servers.

However, over the past few iterations, Magento's developers have worked hard to improve the overall performance. Today's Magento is indeed faster than before, even when taking faster servers into account.

That said, for Magento to perform at the highest levels of performance, there are areas which you should become familiar with. Specifically:

- The Magento EAV methodology
- Indexing and caching
- Server tuning configurations

After all, a faster website improves the customer experience and helps improve your rankings with search engines.

Exploring EAV

Most databases for open source platforms are quite simple in comparison to Magento's. For instance, in the past when I designed e-commerce systems from scratch, I would build one table for products that would contain all the key information relating to that product, such as price, available quantity, description, weight, and so on. I might have related tables to store images, but usually one table existed for products, customers, categories, and so on. The challenge with this traditional approach is that if we needed to add a new product attribute, such as height, that field would have to be added to the `product` table, thereby making previous versions incompatible and complicating any upgrade path.

In order for Magento to be a truly scalable platform, its developers utilize an **Entity-Attribute-Value (EAV)** architecture. This database structure adds a great deal of complexity to the Magento data model, to be sure, but its advantage is its ability to allow an unlimited number of attributes to be added to any core item, such as products, categories, customers, addresses, and more. Today's Magento installs an initial 325 data tables, many of which are related to EAV.

EAV allows developers (and you) the ability to extend any entity's attributes without changing any of the data tables. Let's break down EAV to understand how this works.

 As you go through this chapter, you may want to take an actual look at the tables of your Magento installation. With most hosting providers, you are provided **phpMyAdmin** as a tool for exploring and manipulating your database. If not, you can use any number of available tools, including the free **MySQL Workbench** (http://www. mysql.com/products/workbench/). See your hosting provider for information on how to directly access your database.

Entity

Products, categories, customers, customer addresses, ratings, and reviews are all entities in the Magento data scheme. Each entity has its own entity record in one of the following tables:

- `catalog_product_entity`
- `catalog_category_entity`
- `customer_entity`
- `customer_address_entity`
- `rating_entity`
- `review_entity`
- `eav_entity` (stores product attribute entities)

Each of these entity tables stores very basic information about the entity. For instance, let's take a look at the columns of the `catalog_product_entity` table:

- `entity_id`
- `entity_type_id`
- `attribute_set_id`
- `type_id`
- `sku`
- `has_options`
- `required_options`
- `created_at`
- `updated_at`

These are the only columns required to define any product in the database. Notice that the name, description, and price of the product is not included in this table.

Attribute

Attributes are the names of the various items that belong to an entity. For instance, a product has attributes of price, description, and quantity. Attribute tables don't store the actual value of the item, only its name and its relationship to the entity. That's where **Value** comes in.

Value

If you're following the bouncing ball so far, you can now surmise that **Value** is the actual data of **Attribute**. So, if we use a simple graphic such as the one shown as follows, we can visualize the entire EAV relationship:

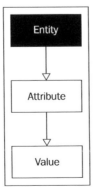

Putting it all together

Let's look at how this works in practice for a product. The product entity is stored in the `catalog_product_entity` table, as described previously. To bring together all the information related to a product, we have to pull in all the various attributes (and their values) connected to the product.

To do that, we look into the `eav_attribute` table. This table connects all the attributes to their respective entities. One column in this table is called `entity_type_id`. This column relates to the `entity_type_id` column in the `catalog_product_entity` table, as shown in the following diagram:

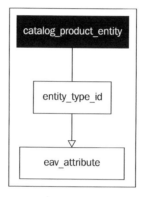

Once the associated attribute for an entity (in this example, a product) is determined, Magento next works to associate the actual value for the attribute. Here's where it gets a bit complicated, but fun!

For each attribute, Magento stores a type for the associated value, such as decimal, integer, varchar, and so on. These are stored in the `eav_attribute` table in a column named `backend_type`. For each type, Magento has a corresponding table, whose name ends in the particular type. The following are the value tables for product entities:

- `catalog_product_entity_datetime`
- `catalog_product_entity_decimal`
- `catalog_product_entity_int`
- `catalog_product_entity_text`
- `catalog_product_entity_varchar`

If a lookup of a product's attribute shows a type of decimal, then the associated value would be found in the `catalog_product_entity_decimal` table. The following diagram illustrates this basic relationship:

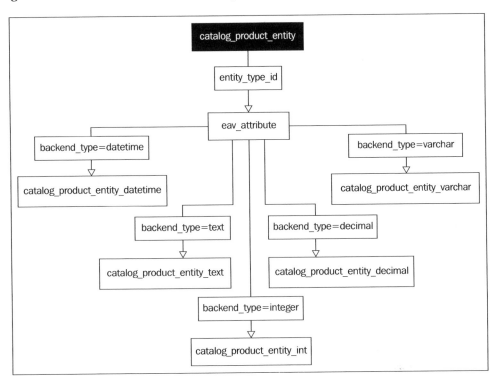

If you take a look at the Magento data tables, you'll now begin to understand the relationship between various entities, attributes, and values.

The good and bad of EAV

EAV is a key feature of Magento that allows developers to extend the platform without changing its core data structure. Imagine that you want to add new functionality that depends on a new product attribute. You could simply add that attribute into the system without adding a single new column to any table!

Unfortunately, there is a trade-off: performance. As you can see, in order to pull in all the information for a product—such as for a product detail page—Magento has to do a lot of calls to a lot of tables within the database. These lookups take time and server resources.

Fortunately, Magento's developers are still a step ahead of us.

Making it flat

Long ago, developers realized that while EAV was a cool way to build extendability into Magento, it added a major hit in performance. All the lookups, particularly for busy sites, can really slow down response times. **MySQL**, the database used for Magento, is a single-threaded database, meaning it can only handle one operation at a time.

The solution was to take all the various relationships and pre-compile them into other tables. In essence, Magento could do its lookups using fewer tables (and therefore fewer SQL statements) in order to get the same data.

If you look again at the data tables, you'll see a number of tables with index or flat in the name. These tables combine the EAV relationships into one table.

In order to take advantage of this feature for categories and products (sales orders are automatically flattened):

1. Log in to your Magento backend.
2. Go to **System** | **Configuration** | **Catalog**.
3. Click to expand **Frontend**.
4. Select **Yes** for both **Use Flat Catalog Category** and **Use Flat Catalog Product**.
5. Click on **Save Config**.

After saving, you should get a notice at the top of your admin page, as shown in the following screenshot:

> ⓘ **One or more of the indexes are not up to date:** Product Prices, Product Flat Data, Category Flat Data. Click here to go to Index Management and rebuild required indexes.

One of the things you will have to do as you add or update products and categories is reindex your site. We'll discuss indexing in more depth in the next section.

Indexing and caching

Today's search engines have started measuring rendering times—the time it takes for a web page to download, including graphics and other files—as part of their ranking algorithms. In the past, we used to concentrate on download speed because so many users were connected to the Internet with slow, dial-up connections. With the proliferation of broadband speeds, most developers eased up on this goal, opting to include more flash animations, larger graphics, and complex JavaScripts. Now, we're moving back to the beginning in order to satisfy Google, Yahoo!, and Bing.

With Magento's complex MVC architecture and database structure, you can have the most efficient frontend design possible, yet still experience very slow download speeds as Magento works to build the pages and query the database. Therefore, to create a site with the lowest download speed, we need to take advantage of two important tools: **indexing** and **caching**. Each contributes its own benefit to your goal of speeding up the page generation process.

Indexing

As your Magento installation grows with products, customers, and orders, database lookups can become slower as the MySQL database has to look among a greater number of records to find the ones it needs. Magento uses a number of indexing tables which provide faster lookups by pre-organizing the data records. However, as your site grows, so do these index tables.

In our discussion on EAV, we talked about flattening the categories and products. In essence, when Magento is asked to index categories and products, it pulls in all the various related EAV data for each and creates records in special tables that contain all the related data in one record. In other words, instead of doing lookups among as many as 50 tables to display all the information on a product, Magento looks to only a handful of tables, thereby gathering the necessary information more quickly.

Flat or not flat

The speed difference when using a flat catalog versus a non-flat catalog is unnoticeable for low-traffic sites, as MySQL can adequately handle requests very, very well. However, as your site grows in traffic, you will notice a wider speed differential. Additionally, if your store hosts thousands of products, you'll certainly appreciate the added speed a flat catalog will give your site.

When Magento creates flat catalogs, it takes the related data contained within several tables and compiles this information into one table. Since MySQL only has to do a lookup on one table—versus many related tables—Magento is able to more quickly pull together the information needed to produce the intended results.

The trade-off is that reindexing a site with lots of products and/or categories can take a long time if you choose to use a flat catalog. For that reason, we generally keep the flattening feature turned off when we populate a new site with products. However, once we go live, we almost always turn on the flat feature to give our sites the fastest rendering possible, even if the initial site traffic is low.

Reindexing

As noted before, if you make changes to your site, Magento will notify you that you need to reindex your site. To do this:

1. Go to **System | Index Management** in your Magento backend.
2. Select the indexes that say **REINDEX REQUIRED**.
3. Select **Reindex Data** in the drop-down menu at the top right of the screen.
4. Click on **Submit**.

Once completed, you will see these indexes with a status of **READY** as shown in the following screenshot:

Caching

While indexing can help speed up database lookups by pre-organizing the data for faster lookups, caching does virtually the same thing for the HTML page components that make up the frontend experience. Caching stores completed pages or parts of pages so that website visitors will be provided with faster downloads.

In a nutshell, caching works like this (see the following chart, also):

1. A site visitor requests a page from your site.
2. Magento first checks to see if the request can already be fulfilled from a cached file.
3. If no cached file exists, or if the cached data is deemed to be *old*, Magento rebuilds the actual file.
4. Magento stores a new copy of the file in the cache.
5. Then, the file is sent to the visitor's browser.

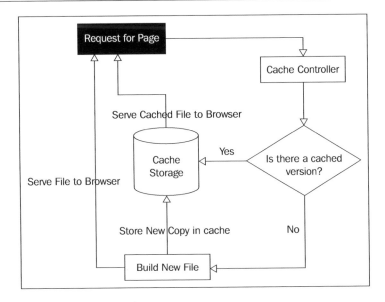

Caching in Magento is accomplished in a couple of ways: with core components (such as modules and layouts) and through full page caching, which stores entire page outputs.

Whole page caching in Community

One of the features that Magento touts about its Enterprise version is **whole page caching**. It is assumed from reading their sales literature that this caching is only available on the Enterprise platform. With version 1.5 of the Community Version, we now have access to whole page caching. Was this an oversight? Did Magento accidentally include this in Community? I'm not sure, but occasionally, I have stumbled across other features within Community that are only mentioned in the features list for the Professional or Enterprise versions. Just count your blessings and enjoy.

Core caching

Every time a page is accessed by a visitor, various modules, layouts, product images, and more are cached or stored for easy retrieval within the /var/cache directory of your Magento installation. If you explore this directory on your server, you'll see thousands of files with strange names. These are the actual pieces of cached data that are delivered to visitors to your site.

Full page caching

Full page caching is just as the name implies: the caching of an entire web page. Imagine the speed boost if Magento did not have to build a new page by assembling dozens of layout and module components, cached or otherwise!

The impact of caching

I've run some tests of sites with and without caching turned on. In almost all our tests, caching improved download speeds by approximately 25-40 percent, depending on the overall load on the server. The heavier the load, the more the benefit since the server is naturally slower in building new pages versus serving cached pages.

This increase in speed, while perhaps not as noticeable to your site visitors, can have a huge impact on how search engines rank your site.

Managing caching

While caching does help speed up page delivery, it does take a bit of management on your part. Caching is controllable in two areas of your backend:

1. Go to **System | Configuration | System**.
2. Expand **External Full Page Cache Settings**.
3. Select **Yes** for **Enable External Cache**.
4. Click on **Save Config**.

Then, you need to set your core cache settings:

1. Go to **System | Cache Management**.
2. Click **Select All** over the first column.
3. Select **Enable** in the upper-right menu.
4. Click on **Submit**.

 Unfortunately, some extensions are not properly designed to participate in Magento's caching system. If you experience problems in how certain content blocks are rendered, you may want to leave the **Blocks HTML output** cache disabled. While this prevents content blocks from being cached, it may be your best remedy if you have any third-party extension of which you're really fond.

Tuning your server for speed

Everyone we talk to who works with Magento is concerned about speed. As we've noted earlier, Magento's complex architecture is simultaneously good and bad. The level of functionality and extendability is practically unparalleled in the world of open source platforms, yet even with proper use of indexing and caching, substantial site traffic can make your Magento site feel like a tortoise on sedatives.

The problem lies, in part, in the fact that developers assume that open source is analogous to quick and easy. The fault is not Magento's: it is what is it—a powerful, yet complex, e-commerce platform.

Therefore, if you want to use Magento to its fullest, it's your responsibility to make sure you have the resources and tools to capitalize on its power. In *Chapter 1, Planning for Magento*, we discussed technical requirements for running a Magento installation. Now, let's discuss some ways of increasing its speed and performance.

Travel with caution

You'll find an almost endless supply of online blogs, wikis, and postings relating to the optimization of Magento. Some offer quick tweaks; others go into elaborate schemas. The challenge when looking for any type of *fix* is knowing what is sound practice and what may be outdated, or simply wrong. The following suggestions are based on what I have found are both within the reach of most developers and that work for the sites we develop and manage. That said, any time you find something you want to try, try it on a test server or your local computer first. *Never apply these modifications to a live, production Magento installation.*

Deflation

Apache web servers have a module called **mod_deflate**. This module, when called by a website, serves to compress files sent by the server. To engage this module, insert the following code into the `.htaccess` file located in the root directory of your Magento installation, replacing what is currently there with the mod_deflate directive:

```
<IfModule mod_deflate.c>
############################################
## enable apache served files compression
## http://developer.yahoo.com/performance/rules.html#gzip

# Insert filter
SetOutputFilter DEFLATE
# Netscape 4.x has some problems...
```

```
BrowserMatch ^Mozilla/4 gzip-only-text/html
# Netscape 4.06-4.08 have some more problems
BrowserMatch ^Mozilla/4\.0[678] no-gzip
# MSIE masquerades as Netscape, but it is fine
BrowserMatch \bMSIE !no-gzip !gzip-only-text/html
# Don't compress images
SetEnvIfNoCase Request_URI \.(?:gif|jpe?g|png)$ no-gzip dont-vary
# Don't compress compressed files
SetEnvIfNoCase Request_URI \.(?:exe|t?gz|zip|bz2|sit|rar)$ no-gzip
dont-vary
# Don't compress pdf files
SetEnvIfNoCase Request_URI \.(?:pdf|doc)$ no-gzip dont-vary
# Don't compress movies
SetEnvIfNoCase Request_URI \.(?:avi|mov|mp3|mp4|rm)$ no-gzip dont-vary
# Make sure proxies don't deliver the wrong content
Header append Vary User-Agent env=!dont-vary

</IfModule >
```

Using **BrowserMob** (http://www.browsermob.com) as our testing source, a configurable product page on our test site (the one we built to use for writing this book) was reduced in size from 452 KB to 124 KB, a 73 percent reduction in the amount of data delivered!

Enable expires

Another Apache module, **mod_expires**, controls how browser caches should treat files they store on users' computers. When you visit a website, your browser caches the results. For files that have not changed since a previous visit, the browser will use the file in the cache on the local computer rather than pull it again from the web server.

The expiration of these cached files can be controlled by your web server. If your server provides no expiration instructions, then your site visitor's browser may assume that the cached information is not good (or is still good long after it is), and fail to pull the best information from your site.

Insert the following within the <IfModule mod_expires.c> directive in your root .htaccess file:

```
ExpiresActive On
ExpiresDefault "access plus 1 month"
```

You can also use a shorter period of time, but generally, you want to allow browsers to use unchanged, cached files for quite a while, thereby lessening the load on your server.

Increase PHP memory

This is one of the most difficult items to change if you're hosting on a shared account, as many hosting providers will not allow you to increase the amount of memory allocated to PHP. The normal default of 64 MB may be sufficient, but if you're expecting a high volume of users, increasing this to 256 MB has produced noticeable improvements for us.

To increase this in your `.htaccess` file, simply place a hash mark (#) before `php_value memory_limit 64M` and remove the hash mark before `php_value memory_limit 256M`.

Increase MySQL cache

This is one configuration you may have trouble implementing as it involves changing a couple of core variables for MySQL. When I started looking more closely at ways of speeding up database lookups, I found that at our hosting provider, MySQL was configured to do lookups without a cache: the query cache and query cache limit were both set to zero.

By doing some research, I found that MySQL queries could be made faster by increasing the total size of the query cache and the query cache limit allowed for any one query. Other developers who had experimented with this suggested at least a limit of 1 MB for the individual query, and a total limit of 64 MB would handle most initial, growing Magento stores. As your store grows, you may want to increase these limits to allow MySQL to take advantage of its own internal caching mechanism.

If you do have the ability to modify your MySQL database—or if you can request a modification with your hosting provider—you should set the `query_cache_limit` and the `query_cache_size` to amounts such as the ones given previously. For specific information on how to set these in MySQL, see `http://dev.mysql.com/doc/refman/5.0/en/query-cache-configuration.html`.

Use a CDN

CDNs, or **Content Delivery Networks**, are servers which host your static or non-dynamic content on very fast servers and networks. For instance, if your images and JavaScript files are hosted on CDN servers, such as the ones provided by Amazon or Rackspace, your Magento server doesn't have to spend time processing and delivering those files to your visitors. Since web servers have limits in terms of the number of active connections they can support for delivering files, allowing other servers to carry part of the load means your server can accommodate more visitor requests.

At present, there is only one Magento extension that adds CDN functionality for images to the Magento platform. The **OnePica ImageCDN** has been successful for a number of Community version installations. For more information, go to `http://www.magentocommerce.com/magento-connect/One+Pica/extension/1279/one-pica-image-cdn`.

At present, there is no capability for using JavaScript CDNs, such as **Google Code**, although you could modify your theme's `header.php` file to include these in your page headers. The problem with this is making sure you get the exact same version as used in your theme.

For instance, if your theme is using jQuery version 1.3.1, you could add the following code to your `header.php` file:

```
<script type="text/javascript" src="http://ajax.googleapis.com/ajax/
libs/jquery/1.3.1/jquery.min.js"></script>
```

Of course, you'll need to remove any existing reference to a local jQuery file. By adding this code as a replacement to your locally served JavaScript file, you're allowing Google's massive network of servers to take some of the load off your own servers.

For information on the Google Code libraries available for your use, see `http://code.google.com/apis/libraries/`.

> **Now you see it, now you don't**
>
> In early versions of Magento Community 1.5, CDN capability was included as part of Magento's "out-of-the-box" features. However, it became almost immediately apparent that their implementation had security issues. Later versions, such as 1.5.1.0, did not include the ability to off-load images to a CDN, and the status of any future re-implementation is not known.

A final word about graphics

In 1995, when I first started building websites, I built to accommodate dial-up connections and small monitors (640 x 480). We took great pains to optimize our graphics by reducing GIF colors or JPEG quality. JavaScript was not used much, if at all, and Flash was not even a consideration.

Boy, have times changed. A majority of the world is now accessing the World Wide Web with broadband connections and web designs are richer and wider. Yet, as we work to make our Magento sites faster, we constantly ask whether we should modify our graphics and designs to be leaner.

The bottom line is results. My feeling is that customers appreciate a very usable interface. Larger photos have proven to be better at selling products than small, pixelated images. Regardless of any speed penalty, we always err on the side of marketing: we design our sites to sell. Therefore, while you want your Magento site to download quickly, don't do it by sacrificing the very reason you're building an online store: to sell products and services.

Summary

Magento continues to amaze me each day I spend building and managing e-commerce sites. There's little debate over the fact that it is both powerful and complicated; both pleasurably configurable and frustratingly massive.

The marketing side of me enjoys the flexibility in design, presentation, and user interaction. The developer side finds satisfaction in learning new ways to squeeze additional performance and functionality from the world's most prolific open source platform.

Hopefully, this chapter has helped you:

- Gain a better understanding and appreciation for Magento's Entity-Attribute-Value data model
- Learn how to use the inherent indexing and caching capabilities of Magento
- Dive into methods of fine tuning your Magento installation for increased performance and shorter download times for store customers

As we near the end of our journey towards Magento mastery, we have one final area to explore in *Chapter 10, Advanced Techniques*.

10
Advanced Techniques

By now, even if you're new to Magento, you should have a newfound appreciation for the power and extendability of one of the industry's most prolific open source e-commerce platforms. We've covered just about everything from installation to extending the platform. Your Magento store, if not already online, is most likely ready from a preparation viewpoint.

However, we're not quite finished yet. You may want to undertake a few more options that can make your installation act more like that of a Fortune 500 company—and less like a hobbyist's experiment in e-commerce.

In this chapter, I will take you through four advanced techniques that I feel any bona fide Magento master should have in their own personal knowledge base:

- Using WordPress with Magento
- Setting up a Staging environment
- Triggering cron jobs
- Backing up your database

You may not wish to undertake all of these now, or later, but at some point, you will find these concepts helpful in turning Magento Community into an enterprise-level contender.

WordPress and Magento

Magento, as we know, is a powerful e-commerce platform. WordPress, on the other hand, is the leading blogging and content management solution, perfect for providing ongoing content about new products, how-to's, and more. Combining the strengths of these two popular platforms can add a new dimension to your e-commerce efforts.

Since both are PHP-based systems, the question becomes, *Can Magento and WordPress run on the same installation?* With the use of third-party extensions, the answer becomes a resounding *yes*!

The FishPig solution

FishPig Ltd. is a British firm focused on developing Magento-based solutions, including a number of extensions I have found to work very well to extend Magento's functionality. **FishPig** offers a free (you have to love the price) Magento add-on for incorporating a WordPress blog within the look and feel of your Magento site. While the instructions for installing this extension are available at `http://fishpig.co.uk/wordpress-integration/`, it's worth covering them here, as you can see from my screenshots how this little gem works. I will be using the same Sample Data installation I have been using throughout this book.

There are a number of niceties about the **FishPig WordPress** extension:

- You can run both your Magento store and WordPress on the same server, within the same root directory.

- Your customers can access your WordPress blog by going to a URL such as `http://www.yourdomain.com/blog`. This means your users' sessions, shopping cart contents, and analytics tracking retain the same root domain.

- You can install your WordPress to use the same database as your Magento installation. You don't have to, but it does make backing up your database easier, as you only have one database to back up.

- Did I mention it's *free*?

Installing WordPress

Of course, if you're going to integrate WordPress, you need to install it on your server:

1. Before you begin (and this is a good habit to adopt), back up your Magento database. Just in case.

2. Using FTP, add a root level folder in your Magento store called `wp`. Make sure the permissions are set to **755**.

3. Download the latest stable version of WordPress at `http://wordpress.org/download/`.

4. Unzip your download and upload the contents into your new `wp` directory.

5. Go to `http://www.yourdomain.com/wp` to initiate the WordPress installation process.

We're going to assume that you know how to install WordPress, or that you'll purchase one of the Packt books covering WordPress. The installation of WordPress is really quite straightforward. If you want to install WordPress on an existing, live Magento store and you have not installed and used WordPress before, I highly recommend that you install WordPress on another server or hosting account first, just to make sure you're familiar with the terms and techniques referred to in this tutorial.

6. If you wish to use the same database as your Magento store, enter the same database credentials as you used for your Magento store in the WordPress installation process. However, to keep your Magento database "pure", you may, instead, want to create a new database for your WordPress installation.

7. Complete the WordPress installation process.

After WordPress is installed, log in to the WordPress backend using the login credentials you entered during installation:

1. Go to **Settings | General**.

2. In the field labeled **Site address (URL)**, enter the full URL that the visitors will use to access your WordPress blog pages. For example, you might use something such as `http://www.sitedomain.com/blog`. Just makes sure it is not the path where your WordPress installation resides. For instance, if you installed WordPress in a directory named `wp`, don't use `http://www.sitedomain.com/wp`.

Installing the FishPig extension

Once you have WordPress installed and initially configured, do the following:

1. Log in to your Magento backend.

2. Go to **System | Cache Management**.

3. Select and disable all the caches.

4. Go to the FishPig extension page at the Magento Connect website (`http://www.magentocommerce.com/magento-connect/wordpress-integration.html`).

5. Get the extension key (version 2.0) for Magento Community. It should be similar to `http://connect20.magentocommerce.com/community/Fishpig_Wordpress_Integration`.

6. Go to **System | Magento Connect | Magento Connect Manager** in your Magento backend.

7. Log in to the **Magento Connect Manager**.

8. Enter the FishPig WordPress extension key into the field labeled **Paste extension key to install**, and click **Install**.

9. Click on **Proceed** and monitor the results in the bottom part of the page.

10. Click on **Refresh** to confirm the installation.

Configuring the extension

You have to admit, that was pretty easy, eh? Now comes the fun part of integrating your WordPress blog into your Magento store. At this point, you have only one demo posting in WordPress, but it's enough to configure the integration before you dive into writing a whole bunch of posts in WordPress.

1. Return to your Magento backend.

2. Log out and log back into your Magento backend (this is important).

You should now see a new menu in your top navigation bar labeled **WordPress**. Let's discuss some of the initial settings which you should be concerned with (if you're like me, you'll eventually enjoy exploring all the various configuration choices).

Database and Integration

If you go to **WordPress | Database/Integration**, you'll first see the light-hearted use of emoticons, as well as green checkmarks, to show that your database is successfully connected and usable by the extension, as shown in the following screenshot:

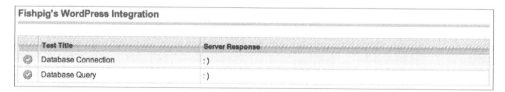

Further down, expand the **Integration** panel. Here, you have the choice of choosing between two different levels of integration:

- **Semi Integrated** means that you have access to the WordPress content from within Magento. This is useful if you want to use a different theme for your blog.

- **Fully Integrated** lends your Magento theme to your WordPress content, and allows you to set the path name for the WordPress portion. The default path is blog, which means if your Magento store URL is http://www.storedomain.com, your WordPress content is accessible at http://www.storedomain.com/blog. Use the same path you used before in the WordPress **General Settings** panel.

For our tutorial, we're going to stick with Fully Integrated, to keep our site looking the same for both, and to provide an easy path for our blog.

Next, expand the **Miscellaneous** panel and enter the full local path of your WordPress installation from the root of your server account. For our installations at **MageMojo** (`http://www.magemojo.com`), our paths look something like `/home/account_name/public_html/wp`. Click on **Save Config** and you should see three more confirmed tests at the top, as shown in the following screenshot:

Fishpig's WordPress Integration

Test Title	Server Response
Database Connection	:)
Database Query	:)
WordPress URL's	:)
Blog Route	:)
WordPress Path	:)

Auto-Login

In order to log in to your WordPress admin backend from within Magento, you can enter your admin login credentials under **WordPress | Settings | WP Auto-Login Details**. Magento will encrypt this information and use it to allow you convenient access to your WordPress backend, where you will create posts for your blog.

At the time of this writing, there's a bit of a wrinkle when trying to use this tool with a multiple store set-up. The FishPig extension only integrates with one WordPress blog per installation. If your stores are related in terms of product focus and content, this might well be a good solution.

Initial peek

The installation and configuration of FishPig's WordPress extension is an example of how a developer can provide a bona fide extension with careful planning and good documentation. Combining two disparate platforms isn't easy.

Using my Sample Data site, the following is a screenshot of what the default store blog looks like with only the initial WordPress installed post:

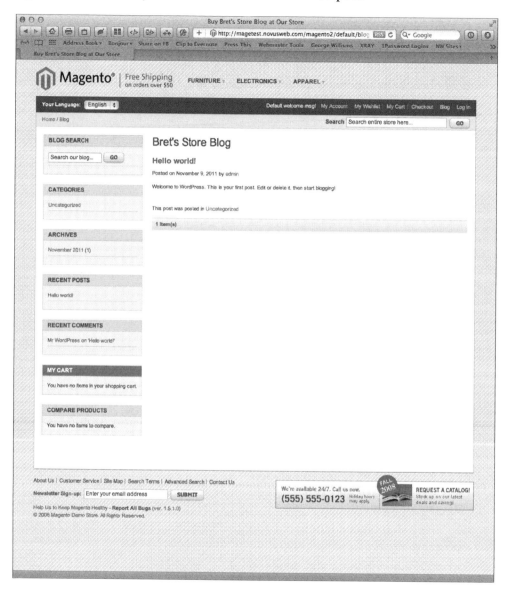

As you can see, the WordPress blog looks like a completely integrated part of the Magento store. If you change stores within your installation, the blog takes on the chosen store's theme as well!

What is equally exciting is that you can add listings of your Magento products into your WordPress postings using shortcodes (abbreviated code that is interpreted into PHP by WordPress). For example, in the sample post shown previously, let's assume we want to include one of our Sample Data products:

1. Go to **Catalog | Manage Products** in your Magento backend.

2. Find a product you wish to profile.

3. Record the product's ID as shown in the left column of the product listing grid.

4. Log in to your WordPress administration backend, find your post, and click to edit.

5. In the content of your post, include this shortcode: `[product id="X"]`, where *X* is the product ID you recorded.

6. Save the post.

Your post now includes a basic listing of the product linked to the full product detail page in Magento, as shown in the following screenshot:

Your visitors can read your blog and click on the product's name to go directly to the full product detail page. If you want, you can even create a unique product template for use in WordPress.

Going the other way

Some site developers may want to use Magento products and content blocks within WordPress blogs hosted elsewhere or outside the Magento store. Searching for Magento at the `WordPress.org` site, you can find several that offer this functionality. However, each one requires a good degree of code revisions within WordPress, well outside the scope of this book. Since you have a good understanding of Magento code elements, if you can likewise take command of WordPress, you may want to take a look at the various Magento-related plugins to see if you can incorporate Magento content into a WordPress installation.

Setting up a staging environment

I know it is so very tempting to install Magento onto a production server account, do the initial configurations, and launch your new store. I also know that if you're only working with one Magento installation, there will undoubtedly come a time when—no matter how careful you are—a buggy extension, an errant piece of code, or a mistyped tag will cause your site to "go dark". You may even experience the dreaded Magento error screen (well known for offering little advice or remedy).

Therefore, if you take no other advice in this book to heart, take this seriously: create a staging environment.

A simple approach

Some developers, particularly those working for large enterprise operations, may want to create an elaborate, versioned, and data-synchronized staging and production setup. If so, you're better suited for Magento's Enterprise solution, than the do-it-yourself Community edition discussed in this book.

For those of us on smaller budgets—who appreciate what Magento Community offers as a robust, yet open source platform—I would suggest that you take a simpler, more rapidly deployable solution. Keep it simple and manageable.

The basic staging setup

There are actually two staging setups I maintain: one for testing and one for client development. The former is used to test new extensions, programming ideas and design concepts, with no particular client use in mind. The latter is created for each client site and, except for the data, is an exact duplicate of the client site in terms of code, extensions, and design.

For client sites, this is my suggestion for a basic operation procedure:

1. Before installing the client Magento instance, install Magento into another server account (you can actually use one account with multiple sub-directories, one for each client staging site). If you're building a new store, you could use the same database for both staging and production in order to keep your configurations in sync. Otherwise, you will need to also manage the configurations in both environments.

2. Install another copy of Magento onto the actual server account that will become the live (or production) store.

3. Complete your install design and configuration onto this first installation. As you complete each major task of your setup, duplicate that task on the production server installation. By keeping the tasks in sync, it will be easier to make sure that every step taken is duplicated for the production installation.

At some point, you will feel you're ready to go live. Guess what? You probably are. If your staging and production installations are in sync, going live is merely repointing the live domain name to your production account, and setting payment gateways to *live* mode.

Don't be tempted to skip

One of the dubious benefits of writing a book like this one is that I get the pleasure of reliving some of my less brilliant moments as a student of Magento as I impart the wisdom gained to you. This is one of those cases.

If you've followed the simple approach mentioned previously, you should have a staging and a production environment that both work successfully. After all, you're not going to do anything to the production installation that you haven't already tried and tested on the staging installation. At least, that's the plan.

But once you launch the production store, there will come a time when you want to take a shortcut. Your client might be pressing to install a new extension they found at the Magento Connect website, or you need to import some new product types the current store has not been using. Regardless, if you skip applying your changes to your staging installation and go directly to the production installation, you'll find that you are about to experience the moment when your heart drops out of your chest as your production store ceases to work as intended. It's another of Murphy's laws.

I only had to do that once—and suffer the client's anguished pleas to "get my store back online!"—to learn my lesson: staging first, then production. Never waiver from this dictum, and you'll continue to successfully please your client, yourself, or whomever is the owner of the Magento store.

Magento Cron

If you're not up on Unix lingo, a **cron job** is a scheduled action that occurs at preset intervals on your server. For instance, Magento can create a new sitemap for your store according to the time interval you configure in the backend.

What is confounding to many new to Magento is that configuring cron intervals for various Magento functions doesn't actually cause anything to happen. The reason is that your server must still be told to run the configured tasks.

Cron jobs are configured by using what are called **crontabs**. These are expressions that dictate how often the server is to run the particular task.

Magento cron jobs

There are a few inherent functions included with Magento that can be run periodically, including:

- Catalog pricing rules
- Sending out scheduled newsletters
- Customer alerts for product price changes and availability
- Retrieval of currency exchange rates
- Creating sitemaps
- Log cleanup

Some third-party modules also include scheduled tasks, such as Google Product feeds. The frequency of most of these can be configured in your Magento backend. For those that aren't, you can find the crontab-style setting for each in the `config.xml` file of each module.

For example, the following is the cron schedule for the function that sends out scheduled newsletters, from `app/code/Mage/Newsletter/etc/config.xml`:

```
<crontab>
  <jobs>
    <newsletter_send_all>
      <schedule><cron_expr>*/5 * * * *</cron_expr></schedule>
```

```
          <run><model>newsletter/observer::scheduledSend</model></run>
      </newsletter_send_all>
    </jobs>
  </crontab>
```

According to this crontab, Magento looks every five minutes to see if any newsletters need to be sent out.

Many of Magentos core modules contain crontab scripts, although some are commented out. The following is a list of Magento Community 1.5 crontabs I have found within Magento, indicating for each whether the script is active or not. To make a script active, simply remove the comment tags surrounding the `<crontab>` code in the appropriate `config.xml` file.

Module	Cron job	Default frequency	Active?
Catalog	Reindex pricing	Every day at 2 a.m.	Yes
CatalogIndex	Reindex the entire catalog	Every day at 2 a.m.	No
CatalogIndex	Run queued indexing	Every minute	No
CatalogRule	Daily catalog update	Every day at 1 a.m.	Yes
Directory	Update currency rates	Controlled by **Currency Setup | Scheduled Import Settings**	Yes
Log	Clean logs	Every 10 minutes	No
Newsletter	Send scheduled newsletters	Every five minutes	Yes
PayPal	Fetch settlement reports	Controlled by **PayPal | Settlement Report Settings**	Yes
ProductAlert	Send product alerts to subscribing customers	Controlled by **Catalog | Product Alerts Run Settings**	Yes
Sales	Clean expired quotes	Every day at midnight	Yes
Sales	Generate aggregate reports (actually there are five configured)	Every day at midnight	Yes
SalesRule	Generate aggregate coupon data report	Every day at midnight	Yes
Sitemap	Generate sitemaps	Controlled by **Google Sitemap | Generation Settings**	Yes
Tax	Generate aggregate tax report	Every day at midnight	Yes

Note that some crontabs run according to values stored in your Magento database. The paths to these settings within **System | Configuration** in your backend are included in this table. Even if these crontabs are active, your backend configuration may need to be enabled in order for these to run.

Triggering cron jobs

For your staging environment, you may want to keep cron jobs from running automatically. Rather, you may wish to have Magento run through its list of scheduled tasks at your command so you can watch for any problems or errors.

To manually run any scheduled jobs, access the cron.php file found in your site's root folder. If your staging server URL is http://staging.yourdomain.com, you would run this script by going to http://staging.yourdomain.com/cron.php in your browser.

For your production server, you'll want cron jobs to run as scheduled around the clock. To do this, you have to create a cron job for your server, telling it how often to trigger Magento's cron tasks. For most servers—Unix and Linux—the cron program operates as a continuous daemon, waiting to take some action according to any programmed crontabs. In this case, we want to have the cron.sh script (also in our Magento root folder) run by the server every few minutes or so. Generally, I set this to run every 15 minutes (we'll see in a moment how you can make sure that jobs set to run every five minutes by Magento are still completed).

Since there are so many different systems and methods for creating crontabs (on Windows computers, these are called **scheduled tasks**), it would be prohibitive to cover all possible scenarios. However, since a significant number of readers will be hosting Magento sites—especially first-timers—on shared servers, you can easily schedule cron jobs using the very familiar **cPanel** interface (you may be using another panel solution, such as **Plesk**; each of these have some type of cron job management tool).

1. Log in to your cPanel server account.
2. Find and click the icon or link to cron jobs.

There are two areas on this screen, as shown in the following screenshot, which are important for our purposes. The first, **Cron Email**, allows you to set an e-mail address to which an e-mail will be sent each time a cron job runs. If you're new to cron jobs, it's a good idea to add your e-mail address here in order to get a confirmation that your cron job is running successfully. After a short while, though, you will want to remove your e-mail address as you will get an e-mail every X number of minutes, 24 hours per day.

The second area is more important. **Add New Cron Job** is where you add the code to set your crontab frequency. Remember, this is not the frequency with which Magento has scheduled certain tasks (more on that in a moment), but the frequency by which you want your server to run the cron script in Magento. The following screenshot shows a typical setting for running the Magento cron script every 15 minutes:

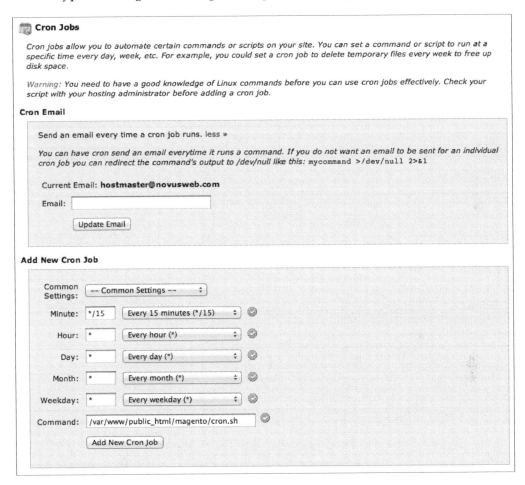

What cPanel has nicely done is to provide drop-down menus offering the more popular settings. Click on any of them to see that you can schedule crons to run every X number of minutes, hours, days, or months. You can schedule it to run only during certain times of the day, days of the week, or months of the year. Cron is an amazingly flexible system.

Tuning Magento's schedules

The `cron.php` script does a number of things when your server cron job runs:

- It executes any scheduled tasks
- The script generates schedules for any future tasks
- Finally, the script cleans up any history of scheduled tasks

The parameters that control this behavior are configured in your Magento backend:

1. Go to **System | Configuration | Advanced | System**.
2. Expand the **Cron (Scheduled Tasks)** panel.
3. For each item, fill in the number of minutes.
4. Click on **Save Config**.

Each field in this panel controls the timing actions of the `cron.php` script:

- **Generate Schedules Every** means that new schedules will not be created more frequently than the number of minutes configured.

- **Schedule Ahead For** sets the number of minutes in which Magento will create future schedules.

- **Missed If Not Run Within** tells the script to run any tasks that were scheduled within the indicated number of minutes before the script ran, but which didn't run already.

- **History Cleanup Every** deletes old history entries in the `cron_schedule` database table. This will help keep the table from growing too large.

- **Success History Lifetime** similarly purges successful entries from the `cron_schedule` table.

- **Failure History Lifetime** does just the same for failure entries.

There remains a considerable debate among bloggers on what values are ideal for this configuration. However, from my observations, there are some principles I follow when configuring Magento cron jobs.

Setting your frequency

Decide the frequency of your server cron job. If you configure your server cron to run every 15 minutes, then you do not need any Magento crontab or cron configuration to be set at anything less than 15 minutes. For example, by default the **Send Newsletter** crontab, as shown in the earlier table, is configured by default to run every five minutes.

If your system cron task runs every 15 minutes, then when `cron.php` is executed, the **Send Newsletter** task is actually run three times, since Magento schedules ahead and looks back to run any scheduled tasks. In other words, if your system cron runs at 10:00 a.m., it will run any tasks that were scheduled to run between 9:45 a.m. (the last time it ran) and 10:00 a.m. Since the **Send Newsletter** task was scheduled to run every five minutes, at 9:45 a.m., Magento scheduled it to run at 9:50, 9:55, and 10:00. The task did not run at those times, but instead were all run at once at 10:00, when your system cron ran.

Therefore, you may want to go back through the various module `config.xml` files (such as the ones in the earlier table) and set the frequency of the jobs to match or be less frequent than your system cron.

Creating compatible settings

Once you have modified any crontabs to match your system cron job frequency, you should now configure the **System | Configuration | Advanced | Cron (Scheduled Tasks)** panel:

- Use the same number of minutes as your system cron job frequency for **Generate Schedules Every**.

- Use the same value for **Schedule Ahead For**. In this way, you are capturing all the upcoming cron jobs Magento intends before your next system cron runs.

- Use the same value for **Missed If Not Run Within**, to run any scheduled tasks that did not previously run during the last system cron.

- Use the same value for **History Cleanup Every**. You can use a larger interval, if you wish, as this is not a function critical to running the necessary cron jobs for your store.

- For **Success History Lifetime** and **Failure History Lifetime**, you can use whatever settings you feel are most important. Generally, when launching a new Magento store, I set the **Failure History Lifetime** for a long time (as much as three days, or 4320 minutes) so that if something seems amiss, I can go into the `cron_schedule` database table and see if there are any failure messages that can help me diagnose the problem. In fact, even if your store is running smoothly, keeping this number large should not grow your database as there will be no failure messages to record.

So, for example, if I set my system cron job to run every 15 minutes, my **Cron (Scheduled Tasks)** panel might look like this:

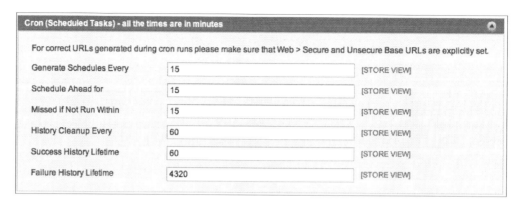

Backing up your database

While we're on the topic of cron jobs, one system cron job you should consider is backing up your Magento database. As usual, this advice is based on hard-earned experience. In the course of working with Magento, and especially if you have clients who have permissions to add extensions and change configuration, you may need to restore the Magento database to a previous, working state.

While most server hosting providers provide backup services, restoring just the Magento database can take a long time, as server backups restore all the files on the server, not just your database. Some providers do provide specific database backups, but to be safe, it doesn't hurt to schedule your server to do your own backups. Additionally, learning how to quickly and easily back up and restore your database will come in handy, since you should always do a backup of your database before installing new extensions or significantly changing configurations.

The built-in backup

Magento does have a backup function in the backend, under **System | Tools | Backups**. While this is one way of backing up your Magento database, there is no built-in restore function. Furthermore, I have had problems in the past using the backup file to restore, due to foreign key conflicts. For extra safety, it wouldn't hurt to use this function to create a backup—especially if you do not have SSH access to your server account—but it is not as easy or quick as the following method.

Using MySQLDump

If you have SSH access to your server, using MySQL's built-in backup and restore functions is both quick and easy. You do need a user and password for your database (which you should have if you installed Magento).

1. To back up your database, access your server via SSH using a terminal program.

2. At the prompt, enter `mysqldump –u [username] –p[password] –h [hostname] [databasename] > [filename].sql`.

 In the previous command, note that there is no space between `-p` and the actual password, but there is a space between the other parameters and their values.

3. In very short order, MySQL will create a file containing a complete restoration script including all of your database records.

To provide some examples for the previous command, let's assume the following:

- MySQL username: `mageuser1`
- MySQL password: `magepassword1`
- Host name: `localhost`
- Name of Magento database: `magento_db`
- File name for the dump: `magento_db`

Using these example values, your command would look like this:

```
$ mysqldump –u mageuser1 –pmagepassword1 –h localhost magento_db >
magento_db.sql
```

To restore your database, a slightly different format is used: `mysql –u [username] –p[password] –h [hostname] [databasename] < [filename].sql`, or, to use our previous examples:

```
$ mysql –u mageuser1 –pmagepassword1 –h localhost magento_db <
magento_db.sql
```

It's as easy as that! And fast.

Setting a cron for backup

Now that you know how MySQL can dump a backup of your database, you can use your server cron to do a dump every night, every week, and/or every month, depending on how fervent you want to be about preserving backups.

Every developer will have their own backup strategies, and so, naturally, do I. While our hosting provider does a complete server backup every night and preserves backups for seven days, I like to augment that with my own database rolling backup strategy:

- Daily backups for each day of the week. Monday's next backup will replace the current Monday backup. Therefore, we will have one backup for each day of the week, but not more than seven at any one time.

- Alternating weekly backups. In essence, we save a backup every other week, so that we have two weekly backups.

- One monthly backup. So far, after 15 plus years of doing this, we've never had to revert to a monthly backup, but I certainly like having it there nonetheless.

One note here: if you can, you may want to consider dumping these to another computer, other than your Magento server. Since our hosting provider does off-site back-ups, I feel quite comfortable backing up our Magento databases onto a local machine at our office. The chances of all three locations: our hosting provider's facility, the off-site back-up facility, and our office all burning down at the same time—I'm sure—are pretty darn remote, especially since all three facilities are spread all across the continent.

To schedule your dumps as crontabs, go to your cPanel Cron jobs panel, as you did earlier in this chapter, and create as many jobs as you feel you need (if you're dumping to another server, you need to, of course, schedule these jobs on the machine to which the backup is to be dumped).

Create a new schedule according to your desired frequency (every day, week, month) and enter your MySQL dump command, as used previously. For the filename, though, use a name unique to the purpose of the dump. For example, for a dump on Monday, you might use `magento_db_Mon.sql`; for week 1, `magento_db_week_1.sql`. In this manner, the next dump for a given script will overwrite the previous dump without filling up your hard drive with dump files.

Summary

After working your way through this book, you've now reached a level of familiarity and understanding that enables you to call yourself a Magento Master. Of course, given the complexity and features of Magento, there's always more you can learn. You should now have enough comfort with Magento that you can freely experiment. After all, one of the greatest features of open source software is that you have the access and freedom to augment the original system to meet your needs.

In this chapter, we have:

- Learned a nifty way of integrating WordPress into a Magento installation
- Discussed a simple method of building and using a staging installation
- Went into a complete tutorial on scheduling Magento cron tasks
- Covered strategies and techniques for backing up your Magento database

With this book in hand, you are most likely close to completing a new Magento store. Launch date is just around the corner. If you've never launched a Magento store before, you're in for a treat now!

11
Pre-launch Checklist

As you've no doubt realized — and one great reason for this book — is that Magento delivers its power as an e-commerce platform by giving you a lot of versatility. This versatility comes at a price, though, most notably in terms of the vast number of configuration tasks and choices available.

Over the years, I have created my own Magento pre-launch checklist to make sure I touch all the important configuration and design points within Magento that are necessary for a live store to operate. If you've read through this entire book, you may have already addressed a number of these items, but having an itemized list to follow will save you a lot of time and give your store owner a great deal of immediate satisfaction.

I've broken down this checklist into the following areas:

- System
- Design and interface
- Sales
- SEO
- Maintenance

In this chapter, we will go over the configurations to review in order to have a successful Magento store launch.

Since so many of the processes noted in this checklist have been discussed in previous chapters, many of the sections in this chapter will refer to previous chapters. Another very good reason to keep your *Mastering Magento* book close at hand!

A word about scope

In *Chapter 1, Planning for Magento*, we discussed the Global-Website-Store methodology. When planning your Magento installation, you set up whether your installation would have one or more websites, each with one or more store views. As you go through this checklist, you need to pay close attention to the scope in which you are updating configurations and designs. For instance, as we discuss Base URLs, take care that your **Configuration Scope** is set at the proper level for the configuration. In other words, if you're updating the Base URL for the entire installation, your **Configuration Scope** is **Default**. On the other hand, if the Base URL applies only to your English language Outdoor Products store view, then set that store view as your **Configuration Scope**.

System configurations

The area of the Magento backend that has the most configuration choices, is within the **System | Configuration** menus and panels. So, let's begin there first.

SSL

Unless your store is using **PayPal Express**, **PayPal Standard**, **Google Checkout**, or another off-site payment processing method (for example, **Authorize.Net Direct**), your store may be taking credit card information on your server. Even if you're not storing the credit card information, you will need to get a **Secure Socket Layer** (**SSL**) Encryption Certificate installed on your server. Depending on the type of certificate you purchase, this process can take from two days to two weeks. It pays to plan ahead on this one: don't wait until the day before launch to try to get a SSL Certificate. Unless you're a master at web server configuration, consult with your hosting provider who can provide you with the necessary encryption keys and installation assistance. For most hosting providers, the installation of a SSL Certificate is outside the permissions of the client (you).

Base URLs

Using the procedures described in *Chapter 2, Successful Magento Installation*, configure your Base URLs for each **Scope** level. You should also review the following panels:

- **General | Web | URL Options**: If you're using a shared shopping cart and/ or a shared SSL, set **Add Store Code to URLs** to **Yes**. To avoid duplication of content (which may hurt your search engine rankings), set **Auto-redirect to Base URL** to **Yes (301 Moved Permanently)**.

- **General | Web | Secure**: If you have your SSL Certificate installed, and you have entered the secure URL as the Base URL in this panel, set both **Use Secure URLs in Frontend** and **Use Secure URLs in Admin** to **Yes**.

Administrative Base URL

Since anyone who has used Magento knows that, by default, the administrative backend of your store is accessible by going to `http://www.storedomain.com/admin`, changing this URL may help keep out the bad guys. To set up a new admin domain:

- Set up your new domain on your server to point to your Magento installation (see your hosting provider, if needed, for assistance).

- Go to **Advanced | Admin | Admin Base URL** and enter the new domain into **Custom Admin URL**. Include any path that is necessary for your store frontend, such as `http://www.newdomain.com/magento`.

Now, you should be able to access your Magento backend using the new domain name. If you have set **Secure Base URL** and **Use Secure URLs in Admin** to **Yes**, then the new domain should automatically change to the secure URL. However, this does provide a convenient and more secure means of isolating access to your Magento backend.

Reducing file download time

Today's search engines are monitoring the speed with at web pages download. The faster the download speed, the better your site is liked by Google et al. More importantly, it makes for a better user experience. Magento helps you by giving the backend administrator the means to combine the CSS and JavaScript files, creating fewer files to download to render a page.

Merging JavaScript files

To combine your design's JavaScript files into one downloadable file:

1. Go to the **Advanced | Developer | JavaScript Settings** panel.

2. Select **Yes** for **Merge JavaScript Files**.

3. Click on **Save Config**.

 You may find, when looking at your frontend source code, that not all JavaScript files have been combined. Some add-on modules add JavaScript links outside of Magento's JavaScript combine functionality. That said, combining most of them using this tool can help reduce the overall download time.

Merging CSS files

The same process can be applied to your theme's CSS files:

1. Go to the **Advanced | Developer | CSS Settings** panel.

2. Select **Yes** for **Merge CSS Files**.

3. Click on **Save Config**.

Compressing CSS files

While there are PHP-based methods for compressing CSS files on your server, an easy approach that doesn't require any special server configuration is to manually compress your CSS files. Let's go through this process using a common CSS file, `styles.css`. We'll use the one in the included Modern theme as an example (you can apply this methodology to all your CSS files).

1. Make a duplicate of the `/skin/frontend/default/modern/css/styles.css` file. If you need to modify the CSS later, it will be easier to navigate. You might call this file `styles-orig.css`.

2. Open the original `styles.css` file; select and copy all its contents.

3. In your browser, go to `http://www.minifycss.com/css-compressor/`. This is a free CSS compressor tool, as shown in the following screenshot:

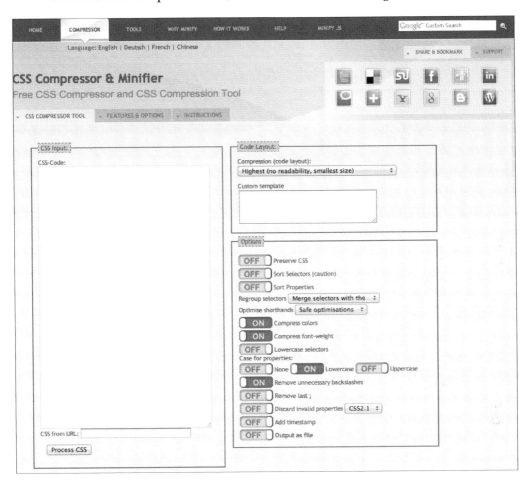

4. Paste your CSS file contents into the **CSS Input** field.

5. You can review the **Options** on the right, but I've found the default settings work fine.

6. Under **Code Layout**, you can choose the amount of compression you prefer. To get the greatest size reduction, choose **Highest**.

7. Click on the **Process CSS** button and the results will appear in the bottom pane of the page.

8. Copy your reduced CSS code and replace the contents of `styles.css` with this new, compressed CSS.

9. Save the changed `styles.css` file to your server.

In this particular example, as demonstrated by the screenshot taken from the bottom of the results output, CSS Compressor and Minifier was able to reduce the Modern theme's `styles.css` file from 84.643 kilobytes to 60.384 kilobytes, a reduction of 28.7 percent. Imagine if you were able to reduce all your CSS files by this factor; your pages will be that much faster to download!

```
Input: 84.643KB, Output: 60.384KB, Compression Ratio: 28.7% (-24259 Bytes) - Copy to clipboard
body{background:#f2f2f2 url(../images/bkg_body.gif) 0 0 repeat;font:11px/1.55 arial, helvetica, sans-serif;
/* Tier Prices */
.tier-prices{background:#f4f9ea;border:1px solid #ddd;margin:10px 0;padding:10px;}.tier-prices .benefit{fon
```

Caching

We went into quite a bit of detail about caching in *Chapter 9, Optimizing Magento*. I mention it here because during development you may have turned off caching to help speed up design and code changes. Take time now to set your optimum caching settings.

Cron jobs

If you haven't already, configure and turn on cron jobs on your installation. Refer to *Chapter 10, Advanced Techniques*, for information on how to trigger cron jobs.

Users and roles

Before you launch, you may want to set up specific users for whomever will have access to your Magento backend. Certain users may only need access to orders and customers. Others may be responsible for product information and pricing.

Before setting up users, you need to set up various roles, or groups of permissions to which you can assign users:

1. Go to **System | Permissions | Roles** in your Magento backend.
2. Click on **Add New Role**.

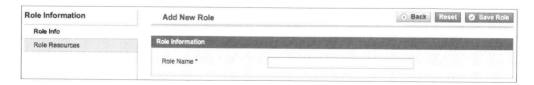

3. Give the new role an appropriate name in **Role Name**.
4. Click on **Role Resources** in the left sidebar.

5. Check the specific permissions you wish to give this role:

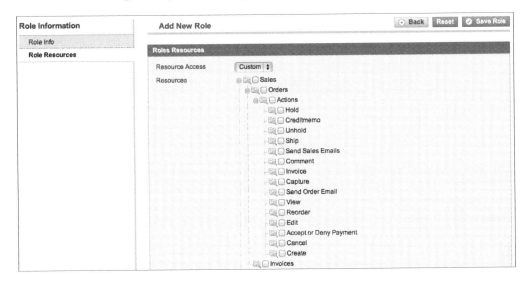

6. Click on **Save Role**.

Once you have your roles set up, you can set up your users:

1. Go to **System | Permissions | Users**.

2. Click on **Add New User**:

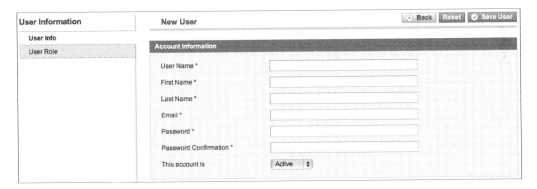

3. Enter the required fields for **User Info**.

4.   Click on **User Role** in the sidebar menu:

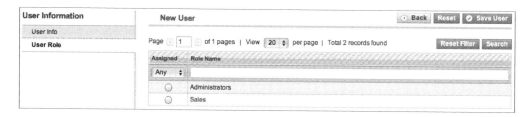

5.   Choose one of the roles you set up previously.

6.   Click on **Save User**.

Once you save the user, an e-mail will be sent to them with the login credentials.

One of the few unfortunate shortcomings of Magento is the inability to restrict a user to a specific website or store. If it's vital that a user have access limited to one particular website, you may need to set up a new Magento installation for each website.

Design configurations

Undoubtedly, you've invested a considerable amount of time creating a frontend design to meet your e-commerce needs. Before you launch, however, there are a few design-related tasks that need to be performed.

Transactional e-mails

Using the techniques described in *Chapter 5, Configuring to Sell*, build and assign the e-mails that will be sent to customers who purchase, register, and subscribe to newsletters.

Invoices and packing slips

The primary thing you need to do for invoice and packing slips is to upload an appropriate logo as a substitute for the default Magento logo. Upload the logo you wish to use for PDF printouts and onscreen views in the **Sales | Sales | Invoice and Packing Slip Design** panel.

 If you want to manage the formatting of PDF printouts in Magento, I can tell you from personal experience that diving into the code files is an extremely time-consuming and frustrating experience. I have found one extension that makes this chore immensely easier: the **PDF Customizer** from Fooman (`http://store.fooman.co.nz/ magento-extension-pdf-customiser.html`). In my opinion, it is one of the best value extensions on the market.

Favicon

Don't overlook this little item! You'd be surprised how many Magento-powered websites I visit that still show the Magento logo. To upload your own favicon, go to the **General | Design | HTML Head** panel under **System | Configuration**.

Placeholder images

For products that have no image, Magento inserts default placeholder images. You can create your own—perhaps with your own company's logo—to use instead of the default images with the Magento logo.

To upload your own versions, go to the **Catalog | Catalog | Product Image Placeholders** panel. If you want to match the same size images used by Magento for its default images, use these sizes:

- **Base Image**: 262 x 262 pixels (used on product detail pages)
- **Small Image**: 135 x 135 pixels (used on category listing pages)
- **Thumbnail**: 50 x 50 pixels (used on the shopping cart page)

404 and error pages

When you first install Magento, a CMS page is automatically created for use when a visitor tries to access a non-existent page. This default page, as shown in the following screenshot with the Modern theme, is not bad, but you may want to update the banner images and, perhaps, provide even better information to visitors as to what they can do to find the correct page:

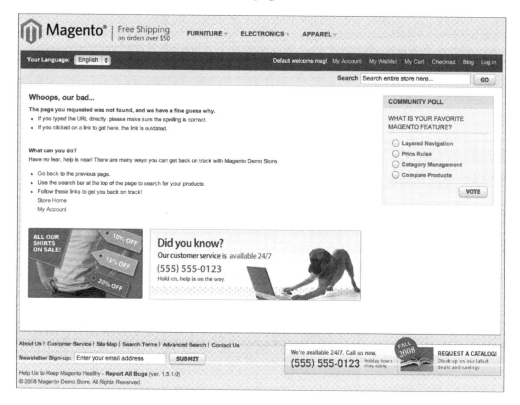

You may want to modify the layout to include a sidebar of categories. It might also be helpful to show your telephone number in large numbers if you want customers to call you for help.

Search engine optimization

Without exception, for an online store to prosper, it has to have customers. Attracting customers comes from a variety of efforts, including search engine rankings. There are lots of SEO-related activities for increasing traffic, from blog postings and backlinks, to product descriptions and reviews. For pre-launch purposes, you want to make sure to do the initial tasks that will add to the SEO arsenal.

Meta tags

If you intend to use **meta tags** as part of your search engine optimization, see *Chapter 7*, *Marketing Tools*, for specific procedural information.

Analytics

In your Magento backend, under **System | Configuration | Sales | Google API** is a panel titled **Google Analytics**. To have Magento automatically include Google tracking code on each page of your site, set **Enable** to **Yes** and enter your Google Analytics ID in the **Account Number** field.

Sitemap

If you did not already do it after reading *Chapter 7*, *Marketing Tools*, configure and activate your Magento store sitemap.

Sales

Before you can begin taking orders on your new Magento website, you need to confirm that you have all the necessary configurations in place.

Company information

In your Magento backend, go to **System | Configuration | General**. Review your settings for the following panels:

- **Countries Options**: This panel allows you to restrict the countries to which you will sell products. Your store owner may have limitations where they can ship and/or receive payments. The **Default Country** sets the default for any country selection drop-down menu.

- **Locale Options**: Use these settings to accommodate the backend users of your Magento store.

- **Store Information**: The values entered here will be used throughout the Magento stores as defaults for name, telephone number, and address.

Store e-mail addresses

Even small online vendors may use different e-mail addresses for different purposes. We often set up multiple e-mail addresses for our client's stores, even if the same person may be receiving e-mails for sales and support. Having separate e-mail addresses helps to segregate e-mails by purpose. Additionally, if the business grows and assigns different people to different purposes, you will have already established different e-mail addresses with the store's customers.

Contacts

The panels on the **General | Contacts** screen allow you to enable the standard **Contact Us** form and set who these e-mails should be sent to. You can also assign a customized transactional e-mail.

Currency

Use the procedures in *Chapter 2, Successful Magento Installation*, to confirm that any necessary currency conversion settings are ready to go.

General sales settings

Under **System | Configuration | Sales | Sales** are various panels that control a rather eclectic group of sales-related functions:

- **Checkout Totals Sort Order**: Using numbers of any value, you can control the order in which various order line items are displayed.

- **Reorder**: Select whether registered customers can use previous orders to generate new purchases.

- **Invoice and Packing Slip Design**: Earlier in this checklist, you uploaded any custom logo designs. You can also enter a company address that you wish to use as an alternative to the company address you entered before.

- **Minimum Order Amount**: In this panel, you can set any minimum order amount (if one is to be enforced), as well as set whether to validate multiple addresses submitted in a multi-address checkout.

- **Dashboard**: If you find that server processing power is low, you may want to set **Use Aggregated Data** to **No**.

- **Gift Options**: For sellers of gift items, such as flowers or jewelry, you may want to allow Magento to include a field for purchasers to use to include a gift message to the recipient. These messages will appear in your order detail page for processing.

Customers

If you plan on having more than one customer group (for example, wholesale, preferred, and so on), set up multiple customer groups according to the process described in *Chapter 7, Marketing Tools*.

In addition, there are a few settings you should review under **System | Configuration | Customers | Customer Configuration**:

- **Share Customer Accounts**: Set whether you want customer accounts shared among all websites or not.

- **Online Customers Options**: The vaguely named **Online Minutes Interval** is used to calculate the number of current customers visiting your store, as displayed under **Customers | Online Customers**. For example, if you set this to 30 minutes, then any customer accessing a page of your site within the past 30 minutes will be considered a current online customer.

- **Create New Account Options**: Use these settings to control how new customer accounts are handled. Reference the transactional e-mails you created earlier for the e-mail-related settings.

- **Password Options**: If you created a new transactional e-mail for sending customers their forgotten password, select it for **Forgot Email Template**.

- **Name and Address Options**: In this panel, you can customize how you capture customer information.

- **Login Options**: Select if you want the customer to land on their Dashboard page or your site home page after logging in.

- **Address Templates**: This is an interesting panel, and one often forgotten when customer address layout issues arise. If you find that any layout in your site is not displaying customer information properly, refer to this page.

Sales e-mails

The **System | Configuration | Sales | Sales Emails** screen provides panels to allow you to choose customized transactional e-mails and sender e-mail addresses for orders, invoices, shipment notices, and credit memos.

Tax rates and rules

In *Chapter 5, Configuring to Sell*, we discussed at length how to configure sales tax rates and rules. Afterwards, you should go to **System | Configuration | Sales | Tax** in your Magento backend for additional sales tax configurations:

- **Tax Classes**: Select whether sales tax is to be calculated for shipping charges.
- **Calculation Settings**: Based on the expectations of your customers and your marketplace, you can configure how sales tax calculations are made and presented in online shopping carts and invoices.
- **Default Tax Destination Calculation**: Since sales tax is generally calculated for sales made for customers living in the taxing jurisdictation of the business, you can set the default sales tax rule for individual store views. Your actual taxing rules will override these default settings.
- **Price Display Settings**: These configurations affect whether products and shipping prices should be displayed with or without including any applicable sales tax calculation.
- **Shopping Cart Display Settings**: Generally, the default settings are appropriate, but you should review how prices, totals, and taxes are to be displayed in shopping carts.
- **Orders, Invoices, Creditmemos Display Settings**: This panel is the same as for the previous panel.
- **Fixed Product Taxes**: Where products are assigned fixed taxes, such as Excise taxes, you can configure how those taxes are to be displayed on the site.

Shipping

Using *Chapter 5, Configuring to Sell*, for guidance, confirm that the shipping methods you want for your new store are configured and ready.

Payment methods

Likewise, you should confirm your desired payment methods. Most can be set in *test* mode during configuration.

Newsletters

Configure and test your newsletter configurations. Refer to *Chapter 7, Marketing Tools*, for detailed information on creating and sending customer newsletters.

Terms and conditions

Later in this checklist, you will set whether or not you want customers to confirm that they have read your site's terms and conditions before completing their purchase. To compose your terms, go to **Sales | Terms and conditions** in your Magento backend. Here you can add the actual text that will be displayed during checkout.

Checkout

Now, let's turn our attention to the checkout process. Go to **System | Configuration | Sales | Checkout**, where you will find the following panels:

- **Checkout Options**: On this panel, you can decide whether or not to use the **onepage checkout** feature, allow guests (non-registered customers) to checkout, and require the customer to confirm they have read and will abide by your terms and conditions.

- **Shopping Cart**: This panel dictates settings for how long quotes should survive, where shoppers are redirected to after adding a product to their shopping cart, and what images should be displayed in the shopping cart for grouped or configurable products.

- **My Cart Link**: Set whether **My Cart Link** shown on each page should display the total number of items in the cart (number of unique products), or the total item quantities (products X quantity of each). For example, if you choose **Display number of items in cart**, a shopping cart with two baseball bats will show *1 item* in the **My Cart** link. **Display item quantities** would show *2 items*.

Products

Aside from the process of adding new products to your store, there are a number of configurations you should review that affect how products are managed and presented. The goal of any Magento store is to sell, and the ease with which customers can shop, as well as the presentation of the categories and products, greatly affects the success of any e-commerce venture.

Therefore, this section of the checklist may be a lengthy, yet necessary, process. There are no set recommendations, either, for most of these settings, as we find different intentions for each site we build. As with all Magento configurations, don't assume each setting's purpose is clear.

Some product categories lend themselves to long listings of products, each on its own line. Other products may be better suited to a grid layout of no more than six products to a page. Magento's immense flexibility means you not only have a variety of presentation options; it also means you have to be willing to experiment and test. And that, my friend, is one of the exciting aspects of configuring a Magento store.

Catalog

The **System** | **Configuration** | **Catalog** | **Catalog configuration** section has, perhaps, the most panels of any section in Magento. I'm going to break each panel down into its own subsection in order to address the many configuration choices.

Frontend panel

This is one panel with which I encourage you to experiment, as it dictates how products are to be displayed when a customer views a category in your store.

- **List Mode**: Set the default category view to **Grid Only**, **List Only**, **Grid by default**, or **List by default**.

- **Products per Page on Grid Allowed Values**: On grid view pages, there will be a drop-down menu to allow customers to select how many products should appear. The values you use here should be a multiple of how many products appear on each row. For the default of three products in each row, use values that are evenly divisible by three to avoid having an incomplete last row.

- **Products per Page on Grid Default Value**: Set the default number of products to display on a grid layout category page.

- **Products per Page on List Allowed Values**: Same methodology as for the Grid Allowed Values, except that you're not concerned with multiples of products per row, since each row only contains one product.

- **Products per Page on List Default Value**: As you can imagine, this is the default number of products that appear in a list view. As with any view default value, this can be a number larger than the smallest number in your list of allowed values.

- **Allow All Products per Page**: If your categories don't contain a very large number of products, you may want to allow customers to select *All* as one of the allowed values. Setting this value to **Yes** will automatically add *All* to the drop-down menu of allowed values.

- **Product Listing Sort by**: Customers can sort views by **Best Value**, **Name**, or **Price**. This selection determines the default sorting of views (see the next section for an explanation of sorting by **Best Value**).

- Use Flat Catalog Category and Use Flat Catalog Product: As discussed in *Chapter 9*, *Optimizing Magento*, flattening category and product records can speed database lookups, thus decreasing page generation times.

- Allow Dynamic Media URLs in Products and Categories: If you want to insert images into product and category descriptions, you may want Magento to use dynamic URLs to preserve the image link regardless of the changes you make to design themes. If you're set on your theme and where you want to store images, set this to No, as it can help reduce the amount of server processing time needed to render description content.

Best Value

Best Value is one of the more misunderstood concepts of Magento configurations, so allow me to explain. If you go to a category detail screen under Catalog | Manage Categories, you'll find under the Category Products tab a list of products assigned to that category. The last column is labeled Position. By entering values into these fields, you dictate a manual sorting order for those products, in ascending order of the position value. For instance, if you want to feature products in a special order, you might enter position values of 10, 20, 30, and so on. The following screenshot shows how I can dictate the sorting order for the Living Room furniture category so that the Chair appears first, followed by the Ottoman, Couch, and Magento Red Furniture Set:

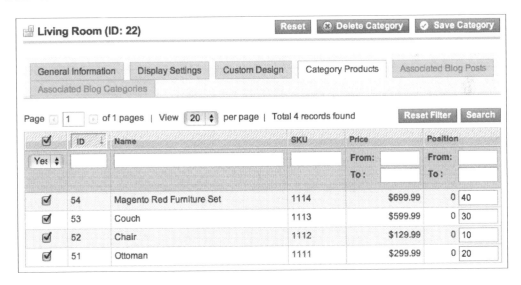

If you do not enter the position values, Best Value sorts by the products' ID values. In this example, if I leave the position values at their default value of zero, these products would appear in this order: Ottoman, Chair, Couch, Magento Red Furniture Set.

Sitemap

This panel does not refer to the same sitemap discussed earlier for search engines. This is the sitemap that Magento automatically generates as a page for your site. On this panel, you can choose whether to show categories in a tree-like, hierarchal structure, and how many lines of categories or products you want to display on each generated page.

Product reviews

By default, Magento allows viewers to submit reviews for products. This panel determines whether non-registered customers — or guests — are allowed to submit reviews for products.

While product reviews are quite popular and a good search engine optimization asset, there may be times when a store does not want to provide product reviews. We had that come up with one of our clients before. To completely turn off reviews, go to **System | Configuration | Advanced | Advanced | Disable Modules Output**. Set **Mage_Review** to **Disable**. Click on **Save Config** and flush your caches. In fact, you may want to review the list of modules under **Advanced | Disable Modules Output** and disable any list your store doesn't need.

Product alerts

The alerts configured in this panel pertain to e-mails that can be sent to customers when product prices or stock availability changes. If you set **Allow Alert When Product Price Changes** to **Yes**, then customers will see a link labeled **Sign up for price alert** on each product page, as shown in the following screenshot:

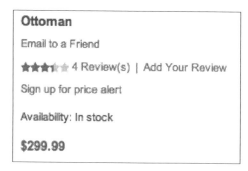

Product alerts run settings

If you have activated your cron jobs, Magento will process any customer-subscribed pricing and stock availability alerts according to the schedule you specify in this panel. You can also receive e-mail alerts if an error occurs while processing.

Product image placeholders

See earlier in this checklist for information on uploading placeholder images.

Recently viewed/compared products

In this panel, you can set how customer-selected recently viewed and compared product lists are handled, especially if you are operating a multi-store installation.

Price

In most cases, a product's price is the same for all websites and stores within an installation. However, there may be occasions where a product has a different price between websites. For example, you might have two websites: one sells products at full MSRP and the other is a discount website, where you want to show lower prices on select items. How you choose product price sharing—globally or by website—also effects how currency conversions are applied to prices.

Layered navigation

In most cases, automatic calculation of price steps in the **layered navigation** sidebar will work fine. However, in some cases, you may want to set your own steps for each store.

Category top navigation

If you want to limit the depth of your top menu category navigation, enter the maximum level you wish. Zero (**0**) means all levels will be displayed.

Search engine optimizations

This panel contains several settings that can affect how well your site is indexed by search engines, such as Google, Yahoo!, and Bing:

- **Autogenerated Site Map**: By enabling this feature, Magento will add a link to a sitemap page for your site.

- **Popular Search Terms**: Likewise, enabling this features adds a link to a page of search terms used in searches on your site. This helps search sites identify links generated by popular searches, and can help in your rankings when those terms are used in the search engines.

- **Product URL Suffix** and **Category URL Suffix**: By default, product and catalog page URLs end in `.html`. You can specify any suffix you wish, but you may also want to have no suffix, as is the common practice for today's websites.

To suffix or not

The debate as to the impact page suffixes, such as `.html` or `.php`, have on search engine rankings has not been settled. The general consensus, though, is that search engines are smart enough today that the page suffix is virtually ignored, as a `.html` page is no longer just a static page; it can be as dynamically generated as a `.php` page. Therefore, the primary determinant should be usability. Is `http://www.storedomain.com/amazing-widget` more readable or remembrable than `http://www.storedomain.com/amazing-widget.html`? Maybe, and maybe not. Personally, I like to leave off the page suffixes, as it makes for a cleaner looking URL. But, if you like having a page suffix, I don't think you can really go wrong as long as it's a common one, such as `.html` or `.htm`. We don't know if Google, for instance, might try to interpret a `.xyz` file differently since the suffix is not common.

- **Use Categories Path for Products URLs**: If you want URLs for products to contain the category name in the path, such as `http://www.storedomain.com/furniture/living-room/ottoman`, set this to **Yes**. As discussed in *Chapter 7, Marketing Tools*, if your URLs are too long, it could work against you.

- **Create Permanent Redirect for old URLs if URL key changed**: During development and setup, I generally set this to **No**, as there is no reason to have Magento create a lot of redirects as you edit product URL keys. However, before launch, you should set this to **Yes** so that future updates will create redirects. These redirects mean that older links still showing in search engines will lead visitors to the correct pages.

- **Page Title Separator**: Enter the character you wish to use in URLs as a substitute for blank spaces. It is generally accepted that a hyphen (-) is better for SEO than an underscore (_).

- **Use Canonical Link Meta Tag for Categories** and **Use Canonical Link Meta Tag for Products**: Search engines—especially Google—can penalize you for duplicate content. In an e-commerce store, categories and products can be accessed through a variety of URLs. For instance, `http://www.storedomain.com/ottoman` and `http://www.storedomain.com/furniture/living-room/ottoman` take the user to the very same page (Magento knows how to interpret both URLs). To Google, these are two different pages, both with the same content. Therefore, Google might penalize your site for having duplicate content, when, in fact, it's not. Canonical Link Meta Tags are, as the name implies, meta tags in your page header that contain, for lack of a better term, the definitive link to the page. That is, if Google analyzes multiple URLs, but each one has the same value for the Canonical Link Meta Tag, then Google understands that these pages are really one and the same, and treats them not as duplicate pages, but simply alternative link paths. An example of a Canonical Link Meta Tag, for our example ottoman, would be `<link rel="canonical" href="http://www.storedomain.com/ottoman" />`, and would be the same regardless of the URL used to arrive at the ottoman page:

Catalog search

Your site will most likely have a sitewide search feature, with a search field somewhere on the page. Allowing your visitors to be able to search your site to find products is one more way you can increase the usability of your Magento site.

- **Minimal Query Length**: This represents the minimum number of characters that are required in order to do a search of your site. While the default value is **1**, I usually set this to at least **3**. Searching for one letter among all the possible categories and products of your site doesn't really make sense. **3** may even be too small. Experiment and find the ideal minimum. In most Magento themes, the search field is auto complete, meaning that once the user starts typing into the field, Magento is immediately searching the database for possible matches, displaying them just below the field (see the following screenshot). This minimum value dictates how many letters are typed before Magento starts this searching process.

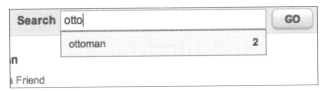

- **Maximum Query Length**: Enter the maximum number of characters you wish to allow for a query.

- **Maximum Query Words Count**: To keep searches fast and efficient, you should have some limit to the number of words that are used in a Like search (see the following).

- **Search Type**: You can specify the type of search you want to use to find matches. If you're familiar with MySQL, you'll understand the difference between **Like** and **Fulltext** searches. This is more important if you allow more than one query word to be used.

Like versus Fulltext

In MySQL, a Like search looks for the entered words as entered within searchable data fields. For instance, if you enter **red ottoman**, a Like search would find all matches where **red ottoman** appears in the field, in that order. A Fulltext search finds all matches where any of the words appear in searchable fields, sorting the results according to how closely they match the entered values. A Fulltext search would find and sort all matches for **red ottoman**, **red**, and **ottoman** appearing separately, and then wherever **red** or **ottoman** appear. This sorting is called **relevancy**. Fulltext searches are nice, but they can be more server intensive than Like searches. They can also display many more results.

- **Apply Layered Navigation if Search Results are Less Than**: Layered navigation can also contribute to the processing time of a search. Generally, if the search results are large, the creation of the layered navigation can take some time. You may want to experiment with this number, particularly if you have lots of products, to find the ideal limit.

RSS feeds

Go to **System** | **Configuration** | **Catalog** | **RSS Feeds** and enable any RSS feeds you want Magento to create.

Maintenance

After setting up a new site, I know it's tempting to leave maintenance issues for a later time. However, before you know it, later becomes yesterday and you may find that not attending to basic maintenance tasks now has become tomorrow's "Oh, shucks!"

Logs

When a new site goes online, you may encounter bugs or other mishaps you did not anticipate. Yes, as strange as it may sound, these things do happen. Sarcasm aside, you should make sure that logging is enabled so you can more quickly pinpoint the cause of any errors. It also helps to review system logs occasionally to see if other things may be happening that don't throw errors, but might be affecting the performance of your site.

Enabling logs

To enable logging, go to **System** | **Configuration** | **Advanced** | **Developer**. Expand the **Logs** panel and set **Enabled** to **Yes**.

Log cleaning

For some reason, the setting for cleaning logs is not on the same screen. Go to **System** | **Configuration** | **Advanced** | **System** and expand the **Log Cleaning** panel. Set your preferences for how long you wish to retain your log files.

Backups

Use the information in *Chapter 10, Advanced Techniques*, to re-confirm that you have set your backup systems in place. This is perhaps the most important pre-launch activity!

Indexing

And last, but not least, re-index the site under **System** | **Index Management**.

Summary

At this point, you should be ready to launch. Of course, the store owner or administrator may still need to add more products and content, but from a developer's point of view, if you have completed the steps in this checklist, your initial work is done.

Congratulations!

I would like to add one more item to the list, though: test. Test, test, test, and test again. Before you go live, have the store administrator, any backend users, and your colleagues go through all possible scenarios. Store owners are always eager to launch, but you cannot overdo thorough testing. It's always better to catch problems before launch than after.

As you've no doubt realized—and one great reason you bought this book—Magento is powerful and complex. Many assume that since Community Edition is free to use and PHP-based, anyone with knowledge of PHP can easily master Magento. We both know that's not really the case. Knowledge of how to apply Magento and the depth of Magento's features and interactions is what will truly make a Magento novice into a Magento master.

Index

Thank you for buying
Mastering Magento

About Packt Publishing

Packt, pronounced 'packed', published its first book "*Mastering phpMyAdmin for Effective MySQL Management*" in April 2004 and subsequently continued to specialize in publishing highly focused books on specific technologies and solutions.

Our books and publications share the experiences of your fellow IT professionals in adapting and customizing today's systems, applications, and frameworks. Our solution based books give you the knowledge and power to customize the software and technologies you're using to get the job done. Packt books are more specific and less general than the IT books you have seen in the past. Our unique business model allows us to bring you more focused information, giving you more of what you need to know, and less of what you don't.

Packt is a modern, yet unique publishing company, which focuses on producing quality, cutting-edge books for communities of developers, administrators, and newbies alike. For more information, please visit our website: www.packtpub.com.

About Packt Open Source

In 2010, Packt launched two new brands, Packt Open Source and Packt Enterprise, in order to continue its focus on specialization. This book is part of the Packt Open Source brand, home to books published on software built around Open Source licences, and offering information to anybody from advanced developers to budding web designers. The Open Source brand also runs Packt's Open Source Royalty Scheme, by which Packt gives a royalty to each Open Source project about whose software a book is sold.

Writing for Packt

We welcome all inquiries from people who are interested in authoring. Book proposals should be sent to author@packtpub.com. If your book idea is still at an early stage and you would like to discuss it first before writing a formal book proposal, contact us; one of our commissioning editors will get in touch with you.

We're not just looking for published authors; if you have strong technical skills but no writing experience, our experienced editors can help you develop a writing career, or simply get some additional reward for your expertise.

Magento 1.4 Development Cookbook

ISBN: 978-1-84951-144-5   Paperback: 268 pages

Extend your Magento store to the optimum level by developing modules and widgets

1. Develop Modules and Extensions for Magento 1.4 using PHP with ease

2. Socialize your store by writing custom modules and widgets to drive in more customers

3. Achieve a tremendous performance boost by applying powerful techniques such as YSlow, PageSpeed, and Siege

Magento: Beginner's Guide

ISBN: 978-1-847195-94-4   Paperback: 300 pages

Create a dynamic, fully featured, online store with the most powerful open source e-commerce software

1. Step-by-step guide to building your own online store

2. Focuses on the key features of Magento that you must know to get your store up and running

3. Customize the store's appearance to make it uniquely yours

4. Clearly illustrated with screenshots and a working example

Please check **www.PacktPub.com** for information on our titles

Magento 1.4 Themes Design

ISBN: 978-1-84951-480-4   Paperback: 292 pages

Customize the appearance of your Magento 1.4
e-commerce store with Magento's powerful
theming engine

1. Install and configure Magento 1.4 and learn
   the fundamental principles behind Magento
   themes

2. Customize the appearance of your Magento
   1.4 e-commerce store with Magento's powerful
   theming engine by changing Magento
   templates, skin files and layout files

3. Change the basics of your Magento theme from
   the logo of your store to the color scheme of
   your theme

Magento 1.4 Theming Cookbook

ISBN: 978-1-84951-424-8   Paperback: 200 pages

Over 40 recipes to create a fully functional, feature
rich, customized Magento theme

1. Create rich, fully featured themes in easy to
   follow steps

2. Customize and localize your themes to make
   them sellable

3. Step-by-step recipes to help you solve problems
   related to Magento theming

Please check **www.PacktPub.com** for information on our titles

Made in the USA
Lexington, KY
10 October 2012